THE RISE OF THE GENOVESE CRIME FAMILY

The Untold Story of America's Most Powerful Mafia Family.

Nutshell Nook

All rights reserved. No part of this publication may be reproduced, distributed, or transmitted in any form or by any means, including photocopying, recording, or other electronic or mechanical methods, without the prior written permission of the publisher, except in the case of brief quotations embodied in critical reviews and certain other noncommercial uses permitted by copyright law.

Copyright © Nutshell Nook, 2024

Table of Contents

Chapter 1 .... **7**
   Origins and Early Years (1892-1931) 7
Chapter 2 .... **19**
   The Luciano Era (1931-1957) 19
Chapter 3 .... **29**
   Vito Genovese and the Changing of the Guard (1957-1969) 29
Chapter 4 .... **39**
   The Era of the "Front Bosses" (1969-1981) 39
Chapter 5 .... **49**
   Vincent "The Chin" Gigante (1981-2005) 49
Chapter 6 .... **59**
   Leadership in Flux (2005-2016) 59
Chapter 7 .... **70**
   The Bellomo Regime (2016-Present 70
Chapter 8 .... **81**
   The Genovese Family's Criminal Enterprises 81
Chapter 9 .... **93**
   Law Enforcement Efforts and Major Cases 93
Chapter 10 .... **104**
   The Code of Silence: Omertà and Genovese Family Culture 104
Chapter 11 .... **115**
   The Genovese Family's Influence on Popular Culture 115

Chapter 1

Origins and Early Years (1892-1931)

The roots of what would grow to be one of the most powerful criminal organizations in American history were planted in the busy streets of East Harlem during the late 19th century when waves of Italian immigrants arrived in the country in search of fresh starts. Giuseppe Morello arrived in 1892, and for many years to come, his presence would change the underground environment.

Born in Corleone, a hamlet in Sicily, Morello carried with him not just hopes for wealth but also the deeply embedded customs of the Mafia in Sicily. Morello's half-brothers Nicholas, Vincenzo, and Ciro joined him within a year of his arrival, creating the core of the group that would soon be known as the 107th Street Mob. This gang of criminals with ties to blood ties swiftly took root in East Harlem and spread into areas of Manhattan and the Bronx.

The Morello gang gained notoriety quickly and brutally. They took advantage of the close-knit Italian immigrant communities, establishing their criminal empire via intimidation, terror, and the promise of safety. In the beginning, they mostly engaged in extortion, protection gangs, and the notorious "Black Hand" plot, a kind of blackmail that frightened Italian-American neighborhoods all around the city.

The Morello gang's aspirations increased with their power. Giuseppe Morello established an important partnership in 1903 that would greatly increase his influence. Ignazio Lupo, dubbed "the Wolf" for his merciless methods, ruled the criminal underworld of Little Italy in Manhattan. This union was cemented when Lupo married Morello's half-sister, forming a powerful criminal organization that controlled a sizable portion of the underground in New York City.

Morello and Lupo's collaboration turned out to be revolutionary. They grew into more complex criminal businesses with their pooled resources and people. They began their daring counterfeiting scheme the same year as their partnership. In collaboration with Vito Cascioferro, a prominent member of the Sicilian Mafia, they set up a network that produced fake $5 notes in

Sicily and transported them into the United States. This operation not only proved the Morello gang's organizational prowess and global reach, but it also made significant revenues.

Law enforcement did not, however, ignore their accomplishment. Italian immigrant turned New York Police Detective Joseph Petrosino launched a thorough inquiry into the Morello family's dealings. Petrosino concentrated his efforts on the extortion racket run by the Black Hand, the grisly "Barrel Murders" (in which corpses were discovered stuffed inside barrels), and the counterfeiting enterprise. In 1909, while searching Sicily for evidence to deport Morello and other mafiosi, he was slain, putting an end to his lifelong passion to overthrow the Morello dynasty.

Authorities eventually apprehended Morello and Lupo. They were taken into custody on November 15, 1909, on suspicion of counterfeiting. Following the trial, Lupo was sentenced to 30 years, and Morello was given 25 years. These were heavy penalties. A power vacuum in the New York underworld was created by this serious blow to the Morello gang's leadership.

Following Morello and Lupo's incarceration, the Lomonte brothers—Morello's cousins—took over as the organization's leaders. From 1910 to 1915, they were in charge of East Harlem. On the other hand, instability and bloodshed characterized their rule. In 1914, Fortunato Lomonte was fatally murdered on East 108th Street. Tomasso Lomonte and his cousin Rose Lomonte met the same end the following year when they were both killed on East 116th Street. These murders demonstrated the erratic nature of power in the criminal underworld and paved the way for further disputes.

There would eventually be territorial issues with other Italian gangs in New York as the Morello family's power grew. During this period, he formed an important partnership with Giosue Gallucci, a well-known merchant in East Harlem and a member of the Camorra, a criminal organization with origins in Naples. Gallucci was an invaluable ally to the Morello family because of his commercial ability and political connections.

But one of the worst feuds in the early history of the New York Mafia would be sparked by this relationship. The murder of Gallucci on May 17, 1915, set off a power war between the Neapolitan Camorra, which was composed of two Brooklyn gangs under the leadership of

Pellegrino Morano and Alessandro Vollero, and the Sicilian Mafia, represented by the Morellos. This battle, which became known as the Mafia-Camorra War, was a watershed in the development of New York City's organized crime.

The violence and far-reaching effects of the Mafia-Camorra War were its defining features. It was a conflict between two criminal cultures more than just a struggle for territory or resources: the looser, more flamboyant Neapolitan Camorra and the more disciplined and secretive Sicilian Mafia. As the fighting raged through the streets of New York, ambushes, retaliations, and killings were routine.

One of the Camorra commanders, Morano, suggested a ceasefire after months of violence. The other Camorra commander, Vollero, had a café on Navy Street where a meeting was set up. But this peace gesture was no more than a bait that would kill. Five Camorra gang members attacked and murdered Nicholas Morello and his bodyguard Charles Ubriaco on September 7, 1916, as they arrived at the café. The disagreement escalated significantly due to this malicious deed, which also dealt a serious blow to the Morello family.

When Morano was accused of killing Morello in 1917, the conflict started to shift. Ralph Daniello's testimony—a Camorra member who had turned informant—was crucial to his demise. Daniello's then-unprecedented level of collaboration with law authorities severely damaged the omertà, the rule of silence that had long protected criminal groups from punishment.

The Mafia-Camorra War was essentially over by 1918 when government enforcement measures destroyed the Camorra in New York. Seeing the writing on the wall, a large number of the remaining Camorra members decided to side with the Morello family. The Morello organization was reinforced by this acquisition of former competitors, which also paved the way for its future dominance.

But for the Morello family, peace did not come with the end of the Mafia-Camorra War. More powerful opponents than the Camorra now awaited them. New York's organized criminal scene was evolving quickly, especially when Prohibition was enacted in 1920. The prohibition on the sale of alcohol provided criminal groups with a plethora of options, and the Morello family moved swiftly to launch a successful bootlegging business in Manhattan.

In the year Prohibition was instituted, Giuseppe Morello and Ignazio Lupo were both freed from jail. But not everyone was happy to have them back in the criminal underworld of New York. During their absence, Salvatore D'Aquila rose to prominence as the head of a formidable Brooklyn Mafia group, and he saw the previous leaders as a challenge to his authority. Another wave of fighting inside the Italian-American criminal underworld began when D'Aquila ordered their killings.

Giuseppe "Joe" Masseria and Rocco Valenti, two individuals who would be crucial to the organization's future, also rose to prominence at this time. The two cruel and ambitious men started fighting for dominance over the Morello family. Their rivalry would lead to a string of bloody encounters that would change the criminal underworld's hierarchy in New York.

During the dispute between Masseria and Valeria, there were many high-profile killings. Masseria's men killed Valenti's important supporter, Salvatore Mauro, on December 29, 1920. On May 8, 1922, Vincenzo

Terranova, a member of the Morello family, was killed by Valenti's crew as payback. After further back-and-forth, Silva Tagliagamba, a further member of the Morello family, was killed by Masseria's group.

On August 11, 1922, the deadly cat-and-mouse game between Masseria and Valenti reached a climax. Masseria's soldiers made a daring maneuver, finding and killing Valenti to end the fighting. The departure of Valenti allowed Masseria to take over the Morello family, ushering in a new chapter in the organization's history.

The family's illegal operations significantly expanded and diversified when Masseria was in charge. Known for his audacious and expansionist plans, Masseria put out great effort to expand the family's illicit gambling, loansharking, extortion, and bootlegging businesses across the state of New York. During his leadership, the American Mafia hired a new generation of criminals who would go on to become famous personalities.

Men like Vito Genovese, Albert Anastasia, Joseph "Joey A" Adonis, Frank Costello, Charles "Lucky" Luciano, and Frank Costello were among these recruiters. These youthful, aspirational mafia offered fresh ideas and vitality to the group. Particularly Luciano advanced fast through the ranks to become one of Masseria's most senior lieutenants, his charm and brilliance identifying him as a potential leader.

But Masseria's growth was not without opposition. He was embroiled in a fierce conflict by the late 1920s with Salvatore Maranzano, a formidable mafioso who had just moved to Sicily to seize control of the Castellammarese family. Eventually, this rivalry would turn into the deadly Castellammarese War, which would completely alter the face of organized crime in the United States.

Taking place between 1930 and 1931, the Castellammarese War was one of the deadliest episodes in American Mafia history. It set up the more Americanized side headed by Masseria against the "old guard" Sicilian mafiosi, represented by Maranzano. Numerous people died in the fight on both sides, and the media and law enforcement paid Italian-American organized crime operations never-before-seen attention.

Many of the younger generation of gangsters, including Luciano, saw that the traditional methods of conducting business were becoming more and more unsustainable as the war continued and the deaths rose. The ongoing violence hurt the company and drew unwelcome attention from law enforcement. Moreover, many of these young mafia members were dissatisfied with the archaic Sicilian customs and management approaches of bosses like Masseria and Maranzano since they were born and raised in America.

In this setting, Luciano started to devise a strategy that would bring the devastating battle to an end and open the door for a new chapter in American organized crime history. Luciano struck a covert agreement with Maranzano after seeing that Masseria was losing the fight. In return for taking over his boss's criminal business and rising to the position of second in command under Maranzano, he consented to destroy Masseria.

The scheme was implemented on April 15, 1931. Masseria received an invitation to eat at Nuova Villa Tammaro, a restaurant on Coney Island. Luciano excused himself to go to the restroom throughout the dinner. Four shooters, Anastasia, Genovese, Adonis, and Benjamin "Bugsy" Siegel, entered the restaurant while he was away and fatally shot Masseria. According to some versions, Ciro "The Artichoke King" Terranova drove the getaway automobile, although Siegel may have taken the wheel because Terranova was too scared.

The Castellammarese War ended with Masseria's murder, and a new era in American organized crime history began. It prepared the groundwork for the development of the Cosa Nostra, or contemporary American Mafia. Following Masseria's death, a series of events led to the creation of the Five Families of New York City and the Commission, an organization that oversaw organized crime and influenced the actions of the American Mafia for many years.

When this turbulent time came to an end, the group that had begun as the East Harlem immigrant communities' Morello gang was on the verge of becoming one of the most powerful criminal organizations in American history. Future generations of the family would operate under the guidance of the lessons they gained in these formative years, which included the necessity for a more organized organization, the diversification of illegal enterprises, and the usefulness of political connections. Now, the scene was set for the emergence of the criminal family that would later come to be known as the Genovese family, led by a new generation of mobsters who were born in the United States and who would propel the group to previously unheard-of levels of influence and power.

Chapter 2

The Luciano Era (1931-1957)

The years 1931 to 1957, known as the Luciano Era, were a pivotal time in American organized crime history. Charles "Lucky" Luciano, a man whose cunning and vision would change the American Mafia's terrain for future generations, was at the core of this turbulent period.

At age nine, Luciano came to the United States with his family after being born in Sicily in 1897 as Salvatore Lucania. He was raised on the impoverished Lower East Side of New York and rapidly became versed in the ways of the criminal underground. Luciano became well-known as a rising star in the city's bootlegging activities during Prohibition in his early twenties.

During the brutal Castellammarese War of 1930–1931, Luciano's rise to power got underway. In this battle, a newer generation of Italian-American criminals connected to Joe Masseria faced up against the established group of Mafia leaders who were born in Sicily and were commanded by Salvatore Maranzano. Once a part of Masseria's group, Luciano recognized a chance to remove both of the traditional bosses and take power for himself and his friends.

Luciano took a risk when he planned Masseria's murder in April 1931. While playing cards at a Coney Island cafe, Masseria was shot. Now that Masseria was no longer involved, Luciano swore loyalty to Maranzano, who proclaimed himself the "Boss of All Bosses." But Luciano's devotion was fleeting.

Luciano responded quickly, seeing that Maranzano was a danger to his own goals. He arranged for a group of Jewish mobsters to visit Maranzano's office in September 1931 and kill him while posing as government officers. After Masseria and Maranzano were taken out, Luciano became the most influential Mafia member in New York City.

More than merely a change of leadership, Luciano's ascent to prominence signified a dramatic transformation in the composition and methods of organized crime in the United States. In contrast to his forerunners, who followed antiquated Sicilian customs and restricted their interactions with non-Italians, Luciano adopted a more contemporary, business-like strategy for engaging in criminal activity.

Among Luciano's greatest achievements was the establishment of the National Crime Syndicate, which was formerly known as the Commission. This ruling board included prominent Jewish criminals like Meyer Lansky and Benjamin "Bugsy" Siegel in addition to the bosses of the main Italian-American crime organizations. The Commission functioned as a venue for resolving conflicts, allocating responsibilities, and coordinating actions among various criminal groups.

The "Boss of All Bosses" paradigm that had governed the American Mafia before was abandoned with the creation of the Commission. The Commission functioned more like a board of directors, with input from each boss on important issues, rather than having a single despotic head. This arrangement made it possible for illicit activity to be more effective and lucrative while also reducing disputes between families.

The newly reconstituted Mafia extended its influence beyond conventional rackets like prostitution, gambling, and bootlegging under Luciano's direction. Through a mixture of bribery, intimidation, and strategic partnerships, the group started to penetrate lawful firms and labor unions to gain influence over a range of sectors.

The waterfront was one of Luciano and his accomplices' primary areas of concentration. Through its control over shipping corporations and longshoremen's unions, the Mafia was able to oversee cargo theft, aid drug smuggling, and extract payments from enterprises that were operating in the ports. For many years to come, the Mafia would profit greatly from their dominance over the waterfront.

Still, Luciano's tenure as America's most powerful Mafia leader was very brief. He was charged with operating a prostitution ring in 1936. Special Prosecutor Thomas E. Dewey, who would become governor of New York and a presidential candidate, led the case against Luciano.

Many prostitutes and madams testified throughout the sensational trial, accusing Luciano of running a large network of brothels. Luciano attempted to cast doubt on the witnesses and present himself as an honest businessman, but in the end, he was found guilty on all charges and given a sentence of 30 to 50 years in jail.

Luciano remained influential in the criminal underworld even after being imprisoned. Through visits from his attorneys and other middlemen, he kept in touch with his colleagues to make sure his interests were safeguarded and the company he founded prospered.

The start of World War II, which would eventually result in an unexpected turn of events in Luciano's criminal career, coincided with his incarceration. The unorthodox proposal that the U.S. Navy made to Luciano in 1942 was received well. Admiral Luciano was asked to help secure the cooperation of dock workers and collect information by naval intelligence authorities who were concerned about possible sabotage at the New York port and wanted knowledge of Axis operations.

Historians disagree on the precise nature and scope of Luciano's contributions to the war effort. According to some reports, he was instrumental in enabling the U.S. troops to invade Sicily by giving them connections and information. Some contend that his contribution was exaggerated and that his main contribution was to maintain worker harmony on the docks.

Whatever the real degree of Luciano's participation throughout the war, he was recognized for his efforts. Governor Thomas Dewey, who had brought Luciano's case 10 years earlier, stayed Luciano's sentence in 1946 in exchange for his deportation to Italy. Dewey's decision was criticized, with some accusing him of striking a deal with the Mafia. Citing Luciano's military service throughout the war and the fact that deportation would be cheaper than incarceration.

Luciano left for Italy on the SS Laura Keene on February 2, 1946. His departure signified the end of his direct authority over the American Mafia, but it did not mean that his impact would diminish. Luciano continued to communicate with his friends in the US from his exile in Italy, giving counsel and arbitrating conflicts.

After being deported, Luciano was instrumental in creating a new center for drug trafficking on a global scale. At the Hotel Nazionale in Havana, Cuba, Luciano convened a gathering of leaders of the American and Sicilian Mafias in October 1946. The vast growth of the heroin trade between Europe and North America was made possible by this meeting, which became known as the Havana Conference.

The American Mafia underwent substantial organizational and operational changes in the years after Luciano's expulsion. Although Luciano's Commission persisted, conflicts and the emergence of new leaders caused a change in the balance of power. Frank Costello, Luciano's close colleague and acting boss during his incarceration, took over as leader of Luciano's previous organization in New York.

Known for his sophisticated manner and political connections, Costello was dubbed the "Prime Minister of the Underworld" and carried on Luciano's more businesslike approach to organized crime. The family became stronger in respectable enterprises and its connections with politicians and other influential people under Costello's direction.

Costello's rule was not without difficulties, however. He almost escaped Vito Genovese's murder attempt in 1957, which was masterminded by the ambitious and vicious capo who aspired to become the family's boss. Costello eventually retired from active leadership of the criminal family due to Vincent "The Chin" Gigante's botched hit on him.

The period Luciano had molded ended with the power struggle that ensued when Costello resigned. After coming out on top, Vito Genovese renamed the group the Genovese criminal family. Unlike Luciano and Costello's more low-key demeanor, this shift indicated a return to a more classic, brutal Mafia leadership style.

Luciano stayed in exile during these turbulent years, observing from a distance as the criminal empire he had created transformed and developed. Through a network of middlemen and front firms, he continued to get a portion of the proceeds from different unlawful enterprises. Nevertheless, when new leaders surfaced and goals changed, his direct influence over day-to-day operations decreased.

In Naples, Luciano lived in relative luxury for his last years, always on the lookout for the police. He participated in a biography and sometimes gave interviews to journalists, but he never fully disclosed the scope of his illegal activity or the inner workings of the Mafia organization he had helped to build.

Luciano died of a severe heart attack at Naples International Airport on January 26, 1962. He was having talks for a movie based on his life with an American producer. With his death, a chapter in American organized crime history came to an official close.

Long after Luciano died, his legacy continued. For many years, the Commission in particular—one of the organizational systems he established—shaped the American Mafia. Mafia activities continued to emphasize building political connections and branching into legal enterprises well into the late 20th century.

Furthermore, Luciano's prediction of a less racially exclusive and more mixed criminal underworld turned out to be accurate. The strict distinctions between Italian, Jewish, and other ethnic criminal organizations became more hazy in the years after his rule, giving rise to increasingly intricate and extensive criminal networks.

Both popular opinions of organized crime and law enforcement tactics were significantly impacted by the Luciano period. Unprecedented levels of public awareness were raised about the reality of Mafia activities during the high-profile trials and investigations in the 1930s and 1940s. Eventually, as a result of this greater knowledge, there were more concerted and forceful attempts to combat organized crime, which culminated in the 1950s Kefauver Committee hearings and the 1970 enactment of the Racketeer Influenced and Corrupt Organizations (RICO) Act.

The life story of Lucky Luciano and the period he defined captures the intricate and often paradoxical aspects of organized crime in the United States in many ways. It's a story about creativity and customs, commercial savvy and violence, intercultural collaboration, and ethnic allegiance. Luciano distinguished himself from his predecessors by his ability to adjust to changing conditions, form alliances beyond conventional lines, and develop new structures for illegal organizations. He also created a pattern that would affect organized crime for years.

Historians, law enforcement officials, and the public are still fascinated by the Luciano period. Books, movies, and television shows have all continued to examine it, providing fresh perspectives on this crucial juncture in the development of American organized crime. Our knowledge of Luciano's influence and the period he influenced is always changing as new records and viewpoints become available, guaranteeing that this period of criminal history will be studied and discussed for many years to come.

Chapter 3

Vito Genovese and the Changing of the Guard (1957-1969)

The American Mafia would be affected by the dramatic change in leadership of the Genovese criminal family in 1957 for years to come. At last, the ruthless and crafty Vito Genovese took over the family that would carry his name. With his ascent, Frank Costello's rule came to an end and a new chapter in the history of one of the most powerful criminal organizations in the country began.

After working as Lucky Luciano's underboss until fleeing to Italy in 1937 to avoid being charged with murder, Genovese had long yearned for the top job. When he returned to the States in 1946, he discovered Costello was now managing the family. Genovese strategically built relationships and bided his time before making his move. His play premiered on May 2, 1957. A young, talented family member named Vincent "The Chin" Gigante attempted to kill Costello outside his apartment complex. Despite failing, the endeavor left a strong impression. Realizing he was in danger, Costello resigned and gave Genovese command.

With the reins of power firmly in his hands, Genovese set out to increase his influence and strengthen his position. Seeking to establish himself as a top boss and address urgent problems confronting organized crime, he summoned Mafia leaders from around the nation to a conference. The Apalachin Meeting was the notorious name given to this assembly.

More than a hundred mafia figures from all across the country gathered at Joseph "Joe the Barber" Barbara's farm in Apalachin, New York, on November 14, 1957. The guest list included members of New Jersey's criminal families, and those from Buffalo, Chicago, Tampa, and New York's Five Families. It read like a who's who of American organized crime. Genovese planned to discuss a variety of illegal activities, such as labor racketeering, loan sharking, and gambling, and to establish his dominance in this arena.

But the conference proved to be a huge failure. The Barbara estate was surrounded by barricades erected by local police officers, who were suspicious of the unexpected stream of costly automobiles with out-of-state license plates. Panic sprang out as the cops moved in. Mob figures escaped into the forest, hoping to avoid being apprehended. Numerous people were taken into custody, including Genovese, who was discovered at a police roadblock with three other guys in a vehicle.

The Apalachin disaster had rapid and widespread repercussions. It was impossible to deny the presence of a national criminal organization for the first time. The event dispelled the misconception that organized crime was just a local problem, compelling federal law enforcement to step up their efforts against the Mafia. Even J. Edgar Hoover, who had long denied organized crime, was forced to consider the facts. The battle on organized crime entered a new phase as the FBI stepped up its operations against the Mafia.

The Apalachin scandal dealt serious damage to Genovese's power and reputation. His leadership skills were called into question, and his judgment was questioned. Other Mafia bosses started to see Genovese as an asset, especially those who had escaped the Apalachin scandal. Among them was the crafty leader of the Gambino criminal family, Carlo Gambino, who saw a chance to destroy a formidable opponent.

Gambino came up with a scheme to depose the Genovese with the help of Costello and Luciano, who were exiled to Italy. They plotted to have him falsely accused of drug trafficking, which is a severe crime with harsh punishments. Genovese was charged with drug offenses in 1958. The evidence of Nelson Cantellops, a heroin addict and dubious police informant, was a major component of the prosecution's case.

Even though the evidence against Genovese was questionable, he was found guilty in April 1959 and given a 15-year jail term. The guy who had seemed set to become the most powerful Mafia leader in America only two years before saw a dramatic turnabout in his life after his conviction. Dreams of dominating the Mafia were shattered when Genovese checked himself into the Atlanta Federal Penitentiary.

Genovese tried to keep his criminal family under his control even after being imprisoned. He depended on temporary managers to oversee daily operations, but his power gradually diminished. The family's activities continued, but without the solid central focus Genovese had offered. During this time, the family's capos (captains) had more freedom to manage their crews and domains with less direct supervision from the top.

With the weakening of Genovese's hold on power, a new family structure developed. In his absence, a "ruling panel" was set up to oversee the family's activities. At first, this panel was made up of underboss Gerardo "Jerry" Catena, acting boss Thomas "Tommy Ryan" Eboli, and Catena's protégé Philip "Benny Squint." Lombardo. The panel system was intended to keep leadership steady and continuous, preventing any one person from amassing undue influence while Genovese was away.

The ruling panel had several difficulties. They had to oversee the family's many illegal businesses while navigating the heightened law enforcement attention that followed the Apalachin Meeting. These varied from more conventional Mafia enterprises like loan-sharking and gambling to more intricate schemes like labor racketeering and infiltration of lawful companies.

Remaining low-key was one of the panel's major tactics. They placed a strong emphasis on prudence and secrecy in all family activities after learning from the Appalachian tragedy. Among the Five Families of New York, the Genovese family gained notoriety for being the most reclusive and difficult to penetrate due to their distinctive strategy.

The family was under increasing pressure from law authorities despite their attempts. Organized crime was the focus of many high-profile investigations and indictments throughout the 1960s. Joseph Valachi's testimony before a Senate committee in 1963 was the most damaging. The first person to openly recognize the existence and inner workings of the American Mafia was Valachi, a soldier from the Genovese family.

Valachi's evidence shed light on the Mafia's organizational structure and workings never before seen. He gave the public the phrase "Cosa Nostra" and described the initiation rite, social structure, and moral code that governed Mafia groups. Valachi's testimony was a PR nightmare for the Mafia and gave law enforcement vital knowledge, even if it didn't directly cause any high-profile indictments.

The betrayal of Valachi was very painful for the Genovese family. It broke the organization's long-standing discipline of omertà (silence), which shielded it from criticism. In response, the family increased the stringency of its recruitment screening processes and increased its level of operational secrecy.

In jail, Vito Genovese's health started to deteriorate as the 1960s went on. Even after he was physically removed from the family's daily activities, he remained a persistent figure in their lives. Many members were afraid of his power and the potential for retaliation, even from prison. This anxiety prevented significant power conflicts or defections and preserved a certain level of cohesiveness within the family.

But with time, Genovese's capacity to guide the family out of jail deteriorated. With increased power came decision-making that impacted the family's destiny for the Ruling Panel. They concentrated on broadening the family's sphere of influence and ventured into more complex criminal activities that were unlikely to draw the notice of law authorities.

The emergence of financial crime was one area. The family became more involved in money laundering, stock fraud, and other white-collar crimes. With less chance of violence and harsher jail terms than typical Mafia operations, these ventures generated considerable profits.

Additionally, the panel sought to increase the family's clout in labor unions. Controlling important unions, especially in the transportation and construction sectors, allowed the family to influence big contracts, blackmail companies, and guarantee its members no-show employment. For the family, this infiltration of organized labor is a reliable and profitable source of revenue.

The family's territorial expansion at this time was another noteworthy development. The Genovese family expanded into New Jersey, Connecticut, and Massachusetts while holding onto its primary power base in New York City. The family was able to enter new markets and generate income thanks to this growth, which strengthened its standing as one of the most powerful Mafia groups in the nation.

The more authoritarian management style of Genovese was quite different from that of the Ruling Panel. They adopted a more cooperative approach to decision-making, seeking advice from important capos before making important choices. This strategy assisted in preserving family harmony and avoiding internal disputes that may draw unwelcome attention.

The panel structure did not, however, come without difficulties. Though they were mostly resolved behind closed doors, power conflicts, and disputes sometimes resulted from the division of authority. The panelists' individual interests and power bases were not always entirely aligned. It took ongoing compromise and negotiation to manage these internal dynamics while presenting a unified face to the outside world.

It became evident that Vito Genovese would not be taking back his position of authority as the end of the 1960s drew near. His health was deteriorating, and during his imprisonment, organized crime had undergone significant transformation. Others were now in charge of the family he had worked so hard to govern, and they were doing it under a new paradigm that was being created by shifting criminal opportunities and rising law enforcement pressure.

Vito Genovese passed away in the United States Medical Center for Federal Prisoners in Springfield, Missouri, on February 14, 1969. The family that held his name saw the end of an era with his passing. The individual who had previously seemed ready to rise to the position of most influential Mafia leader in the United States had passed away in prison, his lofty goals unfulfilled.

Following Genovese's passing, the family had to make a significant adjustment. The man who had given the family its name was no longer even a nominal leader, leaving the Ruling Panel, which had successfully run the family's affairs for ten years, to figure out a new direction.

Rather than designate a single person as boss, the panel chose to preserve the leadership structure they had created. Part of the reason for this choice was to steer clear of the type of power struggle that had marked Genovese's ascent to prominence. It was also a calculated effort to make it harder for the family's leaders to be targeted by law authorities.

The Genovese criminal family found itself at a turning point as the 1960s drew to an end. The days of ostentatious, public bosses like Genovese were coming to an end. A new Mafia leadership style, one marked by flexibility, secrecy, and a more corporate approach to organized crime, was taking its place.

The family's activities would be shaped by the lessons learned during the turbulent years of 1957–1969 for many years to come. The tragic Apalachin Meeting made it clear how important it is to have a low profile and stay away from such gatherings. The Valachi proceedings highlighted the need for unwavering loyalty and stricter member screening. The Ruling Panel's accomplishments proved that a more dispersed leadership paradigm might work.

The Genovese family is now well-positioned to withstand the storm of heightened law enforcement pressure in the next decades thanks to these lessons, which were hard-earned through years of hardships and obstacles. The Genovese family's focus on secrecy and adaptation would help it to preserve its place as one of the most powerful and durable criminal organizations in American history, while other Mafia families would be decimated by high-profile indictments and internal turmoil.

Chapter 4

The Era of the "Front Bosses" (1969-1981)

The Genovese criminal family underwent a dramatic change in organization and methods of operation between 1969 and 1981. After Vito Genovese passed away in 1969, the Genovese family started a new phase marked by the use of "front bosses," an unusual style of leadership. This strategy, which was intended to keep the real organization leaders out of the hands of the government, would govern the family's activities for more than ten years.

Philip "Benny Squint" Lombardo, a man whose power over the Genovese family was inversely correlated with his public image, was at the center of this plot. Lombardo became apparent as the real force behind the crown; he had been an important member of the governing panel throughout Genovese's incarceration. But in contrast to his forebears, Lombardo preferred to rule in secret and never formally assumed the title of boss.

Lombardo chose to stay in the background because he was aware of how organized crime in America was evolving. Law enforcement placed tremendous pressure on Mafia organizations in the 1960s, which resulted in several high-profile trials and convictions. In this new setting, the old paradigm of a highly visible, readily targeted boss was unsustainable.

Rather, Lombardo established a structure of "front bosses"—people who would seem to be guiding the family toward the outside world, but who would hold the true control. This tactic fulfilled many objectives. It provided Lombardo with a buffer from law enforcement scrutiny, disambiguated the family's real leadership structure, and offered disposable figureheads who were willing to step in and take the fall when needed.

Thomas "Tommy Ryan" Eboli was the first of these front bosses. Eboli was an obvious option for the position since he had worked with Lombardo on the ruling panel. Among the underground in New York, he was well-known and liked by other Mafia families. By all appearances, Eboli was the Genovese family's new leader. He was just a puppet, with Lombardo controlling everything from behind the scenes.

Eboli's time as the frontrunner was brief. He was killed in Brooklyn's Crown Heights in 1972. Although the exact circumstances of his death are still unknown, it is thought that his failure to pay back a $4 million debt to Carlo Gambino was a major factor. Typically, the death of a presumed leader would have caused discord in a criminal family. Nonetheless, the Genovese family's business activities carried on almost unhindered, demonstrating the potency of Lombardo's leadership style.

After Eboli died, Lombardo promoted Frank "Funzi" Tieri as front boss. Tieri was a fascinating selection. Within the family, he was a respected and competent capo, well-known for his diplomatic and astute abilities. He was intimately associated with the Gambino family, however, which led some to assume that his appointment was a component of a broader peace accord between the two influential groups.

Tieri took on the role of front boss and became the Genovese family's public face. Besides overseeing the organization's daily activities, he negotiated with other families and attended Commission sessions. It seemed to both rival gangsters and law enforcement that Tieri was securely in charge of one of the most powerful criminal families in New York.

But Lombardo remained the family's general strategist behind the scenes. He was able to operate with impunity because of his low profile, which rendered him almost undetectable to police authorities. Lombardo avoided the social clubs that other mafia members frequented, was seldom seen in public, and mostly transacted business via reliable middlemen. Because of this strategy, he was dubbed "The Quiet Don," a title that well described his style of leadership.

Lombardo oversaw the Genovese family's expansion and diversification of their illicit businesses. The family evolved into more sophisticated kinds of crime, although classic Mafia operations like labor racketeering, gambling, and loan sharking continued to be significant sources of income. Money laundering, insurance fraud, and stock manipulation are examples of white-collar crimes that have grown in importance inside the family's investment portfolio.

Additionally, the family tightened their hold on important labor unions, especially in the shipping and building sectors. The Genovese family was able to influence the granting of lucrative contracts, blackmail contractors, and obtain no-show employment for its members by putting their allies in prominent positions inside these unions. It would turn out that this organized labor infiltration was one of the family's most successful and long-lasting ventures.

A defining feature of Lombardo's leadership was his preference for long-term stability over quick wins. He advised family members to stay out of the spotlight, abstain from needless conflict, and make investments in respectable companies. The Genovese family was able to evade a significant amount of the law enforcement pressure that was being applied to other Mafia groups at this time because of their strategy.

But word of the family's illegal activity wasn't completely lost. Law enforcement authorities began constructing charges against different members of the group throughout the 1970s. Their task was to break through the family's protective shell and obtain information that would enable the leaders to be found guilty.

The family's rigorous observance of the omertà, or rule of silence, made this problem much more difficult. The Genovese crime family stayed mostly together throughout this time, in contrast to certain other criminal families that saw a flood of informants and defections. Law enforcement operations were further thwarted by the members' allegiance, as most of those who were imprisoned opted to complete their sentence rather than assist the police.

The Racketeer Influenced and Corrupt Organizations (RICO) Act presented a fresh danger to organized crime as the 1970s went on. RICO, which was passed in 1970, gave prosecutors formidable new weapons to combat organized crime. The statute gave police the authority to take the belongings of convicted racketeers and to pursue whole criminal businesses as opposed to simply specific people.

RICO had little effect on the Mafia at first. Early prosecutions often failed because prosecutors were still learning how to use the new statute properly. But as the decade went on, the Genovese family and other criminal groups started to face a growing threat from RICO.

One of the first significant Mafia figures to experience the full impact of RICO was Frank Tieri. With several other Genovese family members, Tieri was charged with RICO in 1980. According to the indictment, Tieri was in charge of a criminal organization that engaged in labor racketeering, loan sharking, and gambling.

An important turning point in the history of organized crime trials was the Tieri trial. It was among the first instances of RICO being successfully used on a senior Mafia figure. Prosecutors were successful in assembling a strong case against Tieri despite the family's best attempts to discredit him.

The evidence of Vincent "Fish" Cafaro, a member of the Genovese family who had chosen to assist the police, was crucial to the prosecution's case. Cafaro's evidence shed light on the family's hierarchy and methods of operation. Even though he didn't reveal Lombardo's involvement, his evidence was sufficient to have Tieri convicted.

Tieri was convicted of all charges in November 1980. Being the first Mafia leader to be convicted under RICO law, the conviction was historic. Tieri received a ten-year jail term and a $20,000 fine. But he would never serve his time. Tieri, who was already in terrible condition at the time of his conviction, died in March 1981 of natural causes.

The Genovese family's story ended with Tieri's conviction and eventual death. RICO had shown to be a successful tool in fighting organized crime, and the family was going to have to change to meet this new challenge.

Philip Lombardo maintained solid control over the family during this turbulent time because of his modest profile and his subordinates' devotion. But the Tieri conviction suggested that there was a crack in the carefully crafted façade of the family. Lombardo realized that to safeguard the family's interests against ever-more-advanced police enforcement strategies, a new strategy would be required.

Upon arrival in the 1980s, Lombardo set about organizing his successor. Given his advanced age and personal health concerns, he understood the need to facilitate a seamless handover of power. After decades of service, Vincent "The Chin" Gigante was selected as his successor because of his dedication to the family.

Since he tried to kill Frank Costello in the 1950s on Vito Genovese's instructions, Gigante has played a significant role in the family. Even though the hit didn't work out, Gigante had advanced through the ranks and was now one of Lombardo's most reliable captains. He was renowned for his shrewdness, brutality, and unwavering commitment to the omertà ideals.

Over many years, Lombardo started to progressively hand up power to Gigante. This gradual changeover was intended to preserve the family's stability without drawing excessive attention from the police. Nothing seemed to have changed in how the family operated or was organized from the outside.

The Genovese family had prospered during the "front bosses" period. It protected the family's genuine leadership from public view and enabled the family to function efficiently for more than ten years. Due to the family's ability to withstand the increased pressure from law enforcement in the 1970s and early 1980s, they were able to emerge as one of New York's Five Families, if not the most powerful and stable.

But as the Tieri conviction showed, even this well-designed system was not infallible. Lombardo and Gigante realized that new tactics would be required to safeguard the family's interests in the RICO era as they got ready to relinquish day-to-day control of the business.

Building on the groundwork established by the front boss era, Gigante would create his special method of dodging law enforcement attention. Pretending to be mentally ill to evade prosecution is what became known as his infamous "crazy act," and it stands as one of the most daring and persistent lies in Mafia history.

The Genovese family carried over the lessons learned during the front boss era into this new chapter of its history. The family's operations would remain characterized by their emphasis on secrecy, their use of deception to trick law enforcement, and their preference for long-term stability over short-term gains.

The Genovese family had transformed 1969 to 1981 due to changing circumstances. The family had grown stronger and more resilient due to their ability to adapt to new opportunities and threats under Lombardo's taciturn but firm leadership. The family was ready to take on the responsibilities of the upcoming decades as Gigante readied himself to take charge.

The Genovese family's capacity for innovation and adaptability in the face of hardship was proven during the era of the front bosses. This adaptability, along with the family's enduring virtues of loyalty and discipline, would prove essential in the years to come. The Genovese family's dedication to secrecy and cunning would enable it to hold onto its status as one of the most potent criminal organizations in the country as law enforcement strategies changed and rival families crumbled.

Chapter 5

Vincent "The Chin" Gigante (1981-2005)

The years that Vincent "The Chin" Gigante presided over the Genovese criminal family from 1981 to 2005 are considered to be among the most fascinating and crafty in the annals of American Mafia history. Within the world of organized crime, Gigante became famous due to his unconventional methods and decades-long evasion of police enforcement, which also captivated the general public.

Gigante spent years methodically arranging himself among the family's ranks before rising to prominence. Gigante began his criminal career as a boxer and enforcer for the Genovese family after being born in New York City in 1928. When he tried to kill Frank Costello in 1957 on Vito Genovese's behalf, he became well-known. Even though Costello only received a slight injury in the botched hit, Gigante's image as a devoted soldier who is ready to do the most delicate jobs was solidified.

As Gigante rose through the ranks of the family, he started to develop the character that would characterize his leadership and confuse police enforcement for many years to come. Gigante began acting in public in an increasingly unpredictable manner in the late 1960s. Dressed in a bathrobe and slippers, he would prowl the streets of Greenwich Village, looking unkempt and mentally unbalanced as he muttered to himself. This behavior, which gained him the moniker "The Godfather," was a premeditated attempt to give the appearance that he lacked the mental capacity to manage a criminal organization or face trial.

The "Godfather" tactic was complex and well executed. Gigante would often check himself into mental health facilities, sometimes remaining for long periods. He assembled a group of psychiatrists who would attest to his mental incapacity. Family members would support reports of his declining mental condition, especially his mother and wife. This complex farce was intended to confuse authorities and provide a legal defense against indictment.

Gigante's actions behind the scenes differed greatly from his public persona. He may have looked foolish on the streets, but within the Genovese household, he was a merciless operator. He put in place several procedures to keep himself from becoming directly involved in illegal activity. Family members were not allowed to say his name; instead, they had to rub their chins together, a reference to his moniker, "The Chin." Gigante often communicated via intricate webs of middlemen, making it very difficult for authorities to track orders back to him.

The Genovese family strengthened its hold on power and increased the scope of its illegal operations under Gigante's direction. The family was involved in a variety of illicit operations, such as extortion, gambling, loan sharking, and labor racketeering. Gigante was especially skilled at gaining political clout and financial gain by entering labor organizations. Due to the family's influence over important unions in the shipping and construction sectors, they were able to demand millions of dollars from companies looking for profitable contracts or labor peace.

Among the Five Families of New York, the Genovese family rose to prominence under Gigante's rule. The family was spared the high-profile indictments that destroyed other Mafia factions in the 1980s and 1990s because of his circumspect approach and insistence on concealment. The Genoveses kept a low profile and prospered while families like the Gambinos suffered from internal turmoil and relentless prosecutions.

But in the 1990s, when law enforcement stepped up its attempts to prosecute Gigante, his luck started to run out.

He was charged with racketeering in 1990 when it was discovered that he had rigged bids on window installation contracts for the New York City Housing Authority. As expected, Gigante maintained his long-standing charade of mental ineptitude by showing up for his arraignment in pajamas and a bathrobe.

Years passed during the subsequent court dispute on Gigante's suitability for prosecution. Salvatore "Sammy the Bull" Gravano and Alphonse "Little Al" D'Arco, two former Mafia members who became informants, were brought in by the prosecution. They testified that Gigante was perfectly competent in directing the criminal organization and that his seeming lunacy was an act. Gigante's attorneys persisted in providing proof of his mental illness despite this testimony, including letters from doctors describing his several hospital admissions and apparent hallucinations.

When Judge Eugene Nickerson decided in 1997 that Gigante was mentally competent to stand trial, it was a turning point. Following his wheelchair-bound and often confused appearance in court, Gigante's trial was a media spectacle. The jury remained unconvinced despite his continuing performance. Gigante was convicted on July 25, 1997, of plotting to assassinate other mafia figures and racketeering. The guy who had outwitted law enforcement for decades suffered a devastating blow from the judgment.

An era ended with Gigante's imprisonment in December 1997. Given the seriousness of Gigante's actions, Judge Jack B. Weinstein gave him a comparatively light sentence of 12 years in prison, considering his advanced age and physical weakness. That being said, Gigante's power over the Genovese family was far from gone.

Even imprisoned, Gigante maintained command of the family business. He sent commands to the organization's leadership via his son Andrew. By this arrangement, Gigante was able to keep control of the situation while reducing his participation in overt criminal activity. Daily management of the family's affairs was delegated to a succession of acting panel members and bosses, who all reported to Gigante in the end.

Gigante's ability to manage the family while incarcerated was evidence of his capacity to compel loyalty and the structure he had established. Because of their stringent rule of secrecy and compartmentalization, the Genovese family was able to function efficiently even with their master behind bars. During this period, the family expanded the scope of their illicit activities by including more complex schemes like Medicare fraud and stock market manipulation.

But soon, Gigante's lingering effect from his time in jail caught up with him. Federal authorities charged him in 2002 on additional counts of obstruction of justice and racketeering. According to the accusation, Gigante lied to the court on purpose for decades about his mental health and managed the Genovese family from behind bars.

Faced with overwhelming evidence and the possibility of a protracted trial, Gigante made a surprising choice. He entered a guilty plea to obstruction of justice on April 7, 2003. By saying this, he at last acknowledged that his act of insanity had been a protracted fraud intended to keep him out of trouble. With this acknowledgment, the "Godfather" finally came to an end and one of the most remarkable frauds in criminal history came to an end.

For Gigante and the American Mafia alike, the guilty plea was a bittersweet occasion. Gigante admitted his fabled trick had finally worn thin. For the Mafia, it meant the end of an era of powerful bosses who had dominated organized crime in America for many years after seizing control in the middle of the 20th century.

Gigante's sentence was three years after his plea agreement. His health was gradually deteriorating, and he spent his last years in a medical jail in Missouri. At age 77, Vincent Gigante passed away on December 19, 2005, ending one of the most intriguing periods in Mafia history.

Vincent Gigante left a complicated and varied legacy. He was, on the one hand, a master criminal who commanded a massive criminal organization that was in charge of widespread violence and corruption. Law enforcement was frustrated by his prolonged avoidance of justice, which served as evidence of the difficulties in pursuing organized crime.

Conversely, Gigante's rule signified the final collapse of the traditional American Mafia. His downfall was accompanied by a general reduction in the clout of conventional organized criminal organizations. With more monitoring, stricter rules against racketeering, and a greater propensity for mafia figures to become informants, the strategies that had worked so effectively for Gigante in the past—secretiveness, loyalty, and a long-term outlook—were starting to lose their effectiveness.

It is important to acknowledge Gigante's influence on popular culture. His public image as the mumbling, shuffling "Oddfather" captivated the public's attention and has been often portrayed in television and motion pictures. An enduring aspect of New York City folklore is the picture of a formidable Mafia don strolling about the streets while wearing a bathrobe.

The post-Gigante period has not been kind to the Genovese family. Despite persistent pressure from law enforcement and shifting criminal environments, they have managed to maintain their rank as one of the most potent and elusive criminal organizations in the United States. The family has had to adjust to changing circumstances, such as heightened surveillance of conventional rackets and the emergence of transnational criminal groups.

The way that Gigante has managed to keep the family's leadership out of direct criminal activity has continued to impact how the family runs. It has been difficult for law enforcement to develop evidence against the upper echelons of the family because of the employment of acting leaders and intricate communication systems. But inside the corporation, this strategy has also resulted in power battles and instability.

For the American Mafia, Vincent Gigante's downfall signaled the end of an era. During his rule, the Mafia reached the pinnacles of its strength and resourcefulness, but it also started to lose ground as the main player in American organized crime. Gigante was one of the most fearsome Mafia bosses in history because of his adaptability, guile in avoiding prosecution, and iron grasp on power even when incarcerated.

However, Gigante's collapse also demonstrated how American organized crime and law enforcement are evolving. Eventually, the strategies that had worked so well for him over the previous few decades were no match for prosecutors who were dedicated and equipped with new laws and investigation methods. The Mafia's long-standing lie was finally acknowledged in court, marking a significant turning point in the organization's history.

Both the Genovese family and the larger Mafia have had to adjust to a new reality in the years after Gigante's demise. A harsher reality has replaced the idealized picture of the honest gangster who follows a strict code of conduct and outwits the police. Compared to Gigante's time, today's world of organized crime is more varied, global, and often brutal.

Still, Vincent "The Chin" Gigante's legacy lives on. His narrative still captivates criminologists, law enforcement officers, and the general public. It serves as a reminder of organized crime's resourcefulness and adaptability, the difficulties encountered by those attempting to stop it, and the intricate relationships that exist between criminality, mental health, and the legal system.

Even though Gigante's tenure as the "Boss of All Bosses" came to an end, his influence on American organized crime history endures. His narrative serves as a warning about the corrupting influences of authority, the extent people will go to avoid facing punishment, and the ultimate pointlessness of a life spent committing crimes. The mafia's history and mythology are still heavily influenced by Vincent Gigante, the mumbling, shuffling dons who founded an empire on deceit, even as the organization continues to change in the twenty-first century.

Chapter 6

Leadership in Flux (2005-2016)

The death of Vincent "The Chin" Gigante in 2005 marked the end of an era for the Genovese crime family. For over two decades, Gigante had ruled the family with an iron fist, cementing its position as the most powerful and secretive of New York's Five Families. His passing left a void at the top of the organization, initiating a period of uncertainty and transition that would last for over a decade.

In the immediate aftermath of Gigante's death, the family's leadership structure remained shrouded in mystery. The Genovese family had long been known for its complex hierarchy and use of "front bosses" to shield its true leaders from law enforcement scrutiny. This strategy, perfected under Gigante's reign, continued to serve the family well in the years following his demise.

Daniel "Danny the Lion" Leo emerged as a key figure in the post-Gigante era. By 2006, Leo was believed to be overseeing the family's day-to-day operations, effectively serving as the acting boss. However, his tenure at the helm was short-lived. In March 2008, Leo was sentenced to five years in prison for loan sharking and extortion, dealing a blow to the family's leadership structure.

The imprisonment of Leo created an opportunity for other high-ranking members to assert their influence within the organization. Liborio "Barney" Bellomo, a longtime capo who had previously served time for racketeering and murder conspiracy, was paroled in December 2008 after twelve years behind bars. Bellomo's release sparked speculation about his potential role in the family's hierarchy. While his precise position remained unclear, many believed that Bellomo quickly became a significant voice in the family's decision-making process.

During this period, the Genovese family continued to maintain its reputation for secrecy and discipline. Unlike some of its rival organizations, which had been plagued by high-profile defections and government informants, the Genovese family remained relatively insulated from such threats. This adherence to omertà, the code of silence, allowed the family to weather the storm of leadership uncertainty with minimal disruption to its criminal enterprises.

The family's ability to adapt to changing circumstances was evident in its approach to leadership during this time. Rather than appointing a single, visible boss, the Genovese family opted for a more fluid and decentralized command structure. This approach involved the use of acting bosses, panels of high-ranking members, and street bosses who oversaw specific territories or operations.

One such figure who rose to prominence during this period was Arthur Nigro. Nigro, a longtime Genovese member, was believed to have served as the family's acting boss for a time in the late 2000s. However, his tenure was cut short when he was indicted in 2010 for his involvement in a murder conspiracy and other racketeering activities. Nigro's subsequent conviction and life sentence in 2011 served as a reminder of the ongoing pressure faced by high-ranking mafia figures.

The concept of the "street boss" gained particular importance during this era of flux. Street bosses were typically seasoned capos who were given authority to oversee day-to-day operations in specific geographic areas or sectors of the family's criminal enterprise. This decentralized approach allowed the family to maintain its grip on various rackets while minimizing the risk of a single leadership figure being targeted by law enforcement.

Peter "Petey Red" DiChiara was one such street boss who played a significant role during this period. DiChiara, a longtime member of the Genovese family, was known for his influence in the Organization's Manhattan faction. His ability to function effectively while maintaining a relatively low profile exemplified the family's approach to leadership in the post-Gigante era.

Another key figure during this time was Venero "Benny Eggs" Mangano. Mangano, who had served as the family's underboss under Gigante, continued to wield significant influence within the organization even after his release from prison in 2006. His experience and connections made him a valuable asset to the family as it navigated the challenges of leadership transition.

The family's criminal activities continued unabated during this period of flux. Traditional rackets such as gambling, loansharking, and labor racketeering remained core components of the Genovese family's operations. However, the organization also demonstrated an ability to adapt to new opportunities, including involvement in more sophisticated financial crimes and infiltration of emerging industries.

One notable example of the family's continued criminal prowess came in 2010, when Genovese associate

Salvatore Pelullo was indicted for his role in the fraudulent takeover and looting of FirstPlus Financial Group, a Texas-based mortgage company. The scheme, which allegedly involved several Genovese family members and associates, demonstrated the organization's ability to extend its reach beyond its traditional strongholds in the Northeast.

The family's influence in labor unions, long a cornerstone of its power, remained strong during this period. In 2014, several Genovese family members and associates were charged with extortion and fraud related to their control over a local chapter of the United Food and Commercial Workers International Union. This case highlighted the family's ongoing ability to exploit labor organizations for financial gain, even in the face of increased scrutiny from law enforcement.

Despite the lack of a clear, singular leader, the Genovese family managed to maintain its position as the most powerful mafia organization in the United States during this period. This resilience was due in large part to the family's deep-rooted structure, extensive network of associates, and continued adherence to the principles of secrecy and discipline that had long been its hallmarks.

The family's ability to avoid major internal conflicts during this time of leadership uncertainty was particularly noteworthy. Unlike some of its rival organizations, which had experienced bloody power struggles in the wake of leadership vacuums, the Genovese family appeared to maintain a relative degree of stability and cohesion. This unity was a testament to the strong organizational culture instilled by previous leaders like Gigante.

Law enforcement efforts to disrupt the family's operations continued throughout this period. In 2016, a major indictment targeted 46 alleged mobsters from several crime families, including key Genovese figures. Among those charged were Pasquale "Patsy" Parrello and Eugene "Rooster" O'nofrio, both of whom were alleged to be high-ranking members of the Genovese family. The indictment covered a wide range of criminal activities, including extortion, gambling, and credit card fraud, underscoring the diverse nature of the family's ongoing criminal enterprises.

The arrest and conviction of these high-ranking members presented yet another challenge to the family's leadership structure. However, true to form, the Genovese organization showed its resilience, quickly adapting to these setbacks and continuing its operations with minimal disruption.

As the period of flux continued, younger family members began to assert themselves within the organization. These up-and-coming figures, often the sons or nephews of established Genovese members, represented the next generation of leadership for the family. Their ascension within the ranks was a gradual process, carefully managed to ensure continuity and stability within the organization.

One such rising star was Vincent "Vinny" Esposito, son of the late Vincent Gigante. Esposito, who had long been involved in the family business, was increasingly seen as a significant player within the organization during this period. His family pedigree and deep understanding of the Genovese family's operations made him a natural candidate for a leadership role in the future.

The family's operations during this time were not limited to the New York metropolitan area. The Genovese crime family had long maintained interests in other parts of the country, particularly in New Jersey and Connecticut. These satellite operations continued to thrive during the leadership flux, often operating with a degree of autonomy while still answering to the family's core leadership in New York.

In New Jersey, longtime capo Ludwig Bruschi oversaw the family's interests. Bruschi's crew was involved in various criminal activities, including illegal gambling and loansharking. The stability of these operations in New Jersey provided a valuable stream of income for the family during the uncertain period of leadership transition in New York.

Similarly, the family's Connecticut faction, led by Anthony Megale until his imprisonment in 2005, continued to be a significant source of revenue. The vacuum left by Megale's arrest was quickly filled by other capable members, ensuring that the family's interests in the state remained well-protected.

The period between 2005 and 2016 also saw the Genovese family adapt to technological changes in their criminal operations. While traditional rackets remained important, the family also moved into more modern forms of crime. Cybercrime, identity theft, and online gambling became increasingly important components of the family's criminal portfolio during this time.

This modernization effort was not without its challenges. Older members of the family, accustomed to traditional ways of doing business, sometimes clashed with younger associates who pushed for more technologically advanced methods. However, the family's leadership, whoever they may have been during this fluid period, generally recognized the need to evolve with the times.

The family's ability to maintain its influential position within the American Mafia during this period of flux was due in large part to its vast network of associates and corrupt officials. While the identities of the top leadership remained unclear, the day-to-day operations of the family continued largely uninterrupted, thanks to this extensive support network.

Corruption within labor unions remained a key source of power and income for the family. Despite increased federal scrutiny of union activities, the Genovese family managed to maintain its grip on several important locals. This influence not only provided a steady stream of income through embezzlement and kickbacks but also gave the family valuable political leverage.

The family's infiltration of legitimate businesses also continued during this period. Construction companies, waste management firms, and food distribution networks were among the industries where the Genovese family maintained a strong presence. These legitimate fronts not only provided profit opportunities but also served as effective money laundering operations for the family's illicit income.

As the period of leadership flux extended into the mid-2010s, there were signs that the family was beginning to solidify its hierarchy once again. While the identity of the official boss remained a closely guarded secret, it became increasingly clear that a stable leadership structure was emerging from the years of uncertainty.

Law enforcement sources began to consistently identify certain individuals as key decision-makers within the family. Names like Liborio Bellomo, Daniel Leo, and Peter DiChiara were frequently mentioned as potential candidates for top leadership positions. However, true to the family's tradition of secrecy, concrete information about the exact leadership structure remained elusive.

The Genovese family's ability to maintain its power and influence during this period of leadership uncertainty was a testament to the strength of the organization built by previous generations of leaders. The lessons of secrecy, discipline, and adaptability instilled by figures like Gigante continued to serve the family well, allowing it to weather the storm of leadership transition with remarkable resilience.

As the period of flux drew to a close, the Genovese crime family emerged as a still-formidable force in organized crime. While it had faced challenges and setbacks during the years of uncertain leadership, the family's core strength remained intact. Its vast network of criminal operations, political connections, and legitimate business interests continued to generate significant profits, ensuring that the Genovese family would remain a powerful and influential organization for years to come.

The legacy of this period of flux would have lasting implications for the future of the Genovese crime family. The lessons learned during these years of adaptability and resilience would shape the family's approach to leadership and operations in the face of ongoing law enforcement pressure and changing criminal landscapes. As the family moved forward, it would carry with it the experiences of this challenging yet ultimately successful period of transition, ready to face whatever new challenges lay ahead in the ever-evolving world of organized crime.

Chapter 7

The Bellomo Regime (2016-Present

In 2016, Liborio "Barney" Bellomo emerged as the apparent head of the Genovese crime family, causing a major change in the organization's hierarchy. Following the death of Vincent "The Chin" Gigante, the family's hierarchy had been in upheaval and uncertainty for years, but Bellomo's ascent provided some stability. Born on January 8, 1957, Bellomo has been a well-known member of the Genovese community for quite some time. He was inducted into the family in 1977 as a member of the powerful 116th Street Crew, which was commanded by Saverio "Sammy Black" Santora.

Bellomo faced difficulties on his ascent to prominence. Before being released from jail in 2008, he had been convicted of murder conspiracy, and racketeering. Still, his background in crime and strong ties inside the group made him an obvious option for leadership. From a young age, Bellomo had a solid foundation in the family's activities thanks to his father, a soldier in the family who was close to his previous boss, Anthony "Fat Tony" Salerno.

Bellomo's authority and esteem inside the FBI were shown in 2016, when the agency recognized him as the Genovese family's probable formal supervisor. After years of meticulous observation and information collection, law enforcement agencies—who for a long time had been trying to disentangle the clandestine leadership structure of the most powerful Mafia family in the United States—acknowledged this.

The Genovese family preserved its reputation for discipline and secrecy under Bellomo's direction. The group persisted in doing business at a degree of sophistication that distinguished it from other Mafia families. Bellomo avoided the showy lifestyle that had often drawn attention from law enforcement to previous mafia bosses in favor of a low-key approach to leadership.

Under Bellomo's leadership, the Genovese family's present organizational structure combines conventional hierarchical components with flexible tactics that have been refined over years of dodging attention from law authorities. Bellomo is the boss and sits at the top of the corporation with a small group of reliable people occupying important roles.

Ernest "Ernie" Muscarella took on the role of underboss in the family after demonstrating years of loyalty to the group. Similar to Bellomo, Muscarella is well-versed in the Genovese family's history, having been the capo and acting leader of the 116th Street crew in the past. His promotion to underboss shows Bellomo's faith in seasoned players who have a track record of skill and dedication.

Pasquale "Patsy" Parrello holds the post of consigliere, which is often the third-highest position in a Mafia family. Parrello worked as a capo in the Bronx for years before moving up to this advising position. His background in running several illegal businesses, including an eatery on Arthur Avenue, made him an invaluable member of Bellomo's team.

One intriguing facet of contemporary Genovese family dynamics is the function of the "street boss." Daniel "Danny" Pagano currently holds this role, which acts as a barrier between the family's daily activities and the formal boss. Pagano, who mostly works in the Bronx, Westchester, Rockland, and New Jersey regions carries out Bellomo's directives. Pagano also supervises several illegal enterprises. Bellomo is further shielded from law enforcement investigation by this arrangement, which enables him to retain some degree of independence from the family's illegal businesses.

The family's approach to succession planning reflects its ability to change with the times. In 1965, Michael "Mickey" Ragusa was born and is now the acting underboss. The fact that Ragusa is at the top of the family structure ensures that the younger generation will continue to lead the group when the elder members retire or run into legal issues. The fact that he may take over as underboss shows how forward-thinking the family is in preserving its power structure.

The Genovese family has persisted in a broad range of illicit enterprises under Bellomo's direction, modernizing old-fashioned rackets and investigating new opportunities for illicit gain. The family engages in a variety of illicit activities, such as labor racketeering, loansharking, extortion, illegal gaming, and infiltration of lawful firms.

The Genovese family's participation in labor unions is still one of the key areas of criminal activity. The family has long held sway over several unions, especially those in the building and waterfront sectors. The group may extort companies, rig contracts, and pilfer money from union coffers thanks to its power. Widespread Genovese family participation in unions including the International Longshoremen's Association and several locals of the construction workers' unions has been revealed by federal investigations in recent years.

The family's gaming businesses have changed as technology has advanced. Although the Genovese family still operates conventional street-level bookmakers, they have branched out into internet gaming sites. These digital businesses have a worldwide reach, which makes it harder for law authorities to find and stop the flow of money used for illegal gambling. The family has also been linked to plans to manipulate offshore betting websites to increase revenues while lowering the possibility of being discovered.

Under Bellomo's rule, loansharking remained a profitable business for the Genovese family. The group lends money at exorbitant interest rates to people and companies who are unable to find other sources of funding. The family can take advantage of weak people and communities because these loans often carry an implied threat of violence if payments are not made. The family has a history of preying on small company owners who are suffering due to economic downturns. They typically make predatory loans that give the family power over the firms.

One of the key components of the Genovese family's criminal history is still extortion. The group still demands "protection" fees from companies operating inside its borders, especially in sectors like food distribution, waste management, and construction. Despite intensified law enforcement attempts to fight organized crime, the family can perpetuate these extortion rackets because of its reputation for brutality and its deep-rooted influence in specific neighborhoods.

Under Bellomo's direction, the Genovese family's role in white-collar crime has become more intricate. The group has been linked to intricate financial fraud schemes, including money laundering, mortgage fraud, and securities fraud. These operations often include the use of offshore accounts, shell corporations, and other techniques to hide the money's true source.

August 2020 saw the occurrence of a noteworthy case that demonstrates the family's participation in financial crimes. Christopher Chierchio, a soldier from Genoa, and a number of his friends were charged with conspiring to swindle lottery winners of $80 million. The indictment revealed the family's capacity to take advantage of even apparently legal financial possibilities for illegal gain by accusing Chierchio and his accomplices of exploiting their roles as financial consultants to drain money from the investments of the prize winners.

The Genovese family's crimes are not only financial and labor-related. The group still engages in more conventional mafia activities, such as trafficking illegal drugs. Although the family has always avoided becoming directly involved in the drug trade, preferring to impose taxes on independent dealers who operate inside their borders, more recent investigations have shown the family's involvement in drug distribution networks.

Elio Albanese and Carmine Russo, two soldiers from Genoa, were accused in November 2022 of their roles in a plot to acquire and distribute oxycodone tablets. The family's apparent ability to adjust to shifting drug markets and take advantage of the opioid epidemic for financial gain is shown by the operation, which reportedly entailed obtaining pills from a doctor in Midtown Manhattan and selling them on Staten Island.

The Genovese family has continued to have holdings in respectable companies throughout the Bellomo government, often using these firms as fronts for illicit activity or as a way to launder money. The family has a history of controlling businesses in sectors including construction, food distribution, waste management, and private sanitation. These seemingly legitimate fronts shield illegal activities and provide the family access to a variety of economic sectors.

Bellomo's family has continued to engage in illegal activity, but his leadership style has been defined by a calculated attempt to evade police authorities. The group still places a strong focus on discipline and secrecy, and its members are expected to uphold the omertà, or silence, rule. Because of this commitment to traditional mafia values, it has been difficult for law enforcement to infiltrate the highest levels of the family's leadership hierarchy.

The Genovese family was nonetheless under police pressure. There have been some high-profile indictments and convictions of family members and colleagues throughout Bellomo's reign. From troops to senior capos, several echelons of the organization have been the subject of these judicial activities.

An indictment accusing capos Nicholas Calisi and Ralph Balsamo, soldiers Michael Messina and John Campanella, and associates Michael Poli and Thomas Poli of racketeering conspiracy including illicit gambling and extortion was served in April 2022. This was one of the case's major developments. The long-term nature of the family's illegal activities was highlighted by the indictment's allegations that the defendants had been running a criminal organization from at least 2011.

The family's tenacity in the face of these legal problems is a credit to Bellomo's guidance and the deeply ingrained structure of the firm. The family has shown the capacity to rapidly adjust when important members are put behind bars, elevating other people to take over open roles and maintaining the ongoing illegal activities.

The Genovese family has continued to have a significant amount of power within the broader American organized crime scene thanks to Bellomo's rule. The family's influence goes beyond its customary strongholds in New York and New Jersey since it is still regarded as one of the most powerful and stable criminal organizations in the nation.

For example, the family's Connecticut businesses continue to generate a significant amount of income. The Genovese community in the state's loansharking and gambling industries has endured, adjusting to shifting social and legal environments. The family's capacity to project influence outside of the Northeast is further shown by the earnings it continues to make from its holdings in Florida and other states.

The Genovese family has continued to develop ties with various criminal groups, both within and outside the Italian-American mafia, under Bellomo's direction. Collaborative endeavors with other criminal organizations are typical, especially in extensive operations necessitating the sharing of resources and knowledge. To safeguard the Genovese family's interests and preserve its dominating position, these partnerships are meticulously handled.

The Bellomo government has always been selective and cautious in its membership and recruiting practices. The family still values loyalty and familial ties in its recruits, often giving preference to those who have been close to current members for a long time. This strategy lessens the possibility of law enforcement infiltration while preserving the cohesiveness of the family unit.

But the family has also shown a readiness to modify its requirements for membership in response to evolving circumstances. The need to bring people with specialized knowledge has been acknowledged, especially in fields like financial fraud and cybercrime. The Genovese family has been able to maintain their criminal edge in an underworld that is always changing because they combine traditional ideals and contemporary needs.

Under Bellomo's direction, the Genovese family is presented with both possibilities and problems as it advances. The family's hegemony might be threatened by the persistent pressure from law enforcement, changing economic circumstances, and the emergence of new criminal businesses. The Genovese family is expected to remain a powerful force in organized crime for some time to come, based on the organization's proven adaptability, enduring influence across a wide range of businesses, and dedication to its founding ideals.

Chapter 8

The Genovese Family's Criminal Enterprises

Long regarded as the most potent and significant of New York's Five Families, the Genovese crime family has retained its hegemonic status by engaging in a wide range of illicit activities. Three main pillars support their activities: loan sharking combined with extortion, gaming enterprises, and labor racketeering. The organization has made enormous profits from these endeavors, and they have also strengthened its position of power over many facets of the economy and society.

For many years, the Genovese family's business model has been based mostly on labor racketeering. The family has long been involved in labor union infiltration. In the years after World War II, their influence grew significantly. The Genovese family has achieved significant influence over important economic sectors in New York City and worldwide via control of key unions, notably in the waste management, transportation, and construction industries.

The family's dominance over International Longshoremen's Association (ILA) residents on the waterfronts of New York and New Jersey is among the most well-known instances of labor racketeering. The Genovese family and other mafia groups controlled recruiting procedures, embezzled union money, and extracted payments from shipping corporations for years, putting a grip on the industry. This authority not only gave the family a reliable source of money but also made it possible for them to support other illegal operations, including cargo theft and drug smuggling.

The family's power was not limited to the docks. Construction unions under Genovese influence were instrumental in several of New York City's major building projects. The family was able to rig contracts, dominate important unions like the Cement and Concrete Workers Union, and siphon off earnings from massive building projects. It was sometimes stated that not a single yard of concrete could be poured in New York City without the mafia receiving a share due to this influence.

Genovese family labor racketeering has also made the waste management sector a prominent target. The family was able to establish virtual monopolies in certain places by controlling garbage-carrying firms and teamsters' unions. This allowed them to raise costs for businesses and governments while abusing their position to profit and committing environmental breaches. The scope of the family's activities was evident in their influence over garbage management, which stretched beyond New York City into suburban regions and even adjacent states.

The Genovese family's strategy for combating labor racketeering has changed over time in reaction to heightened police attention and shifting financial circumstances. Although overt acts of violence and intimidation have decreased in frequency, the family has adjusted by using more complex forms of control. To keep their hold over unions and businesses, they have been known to use front firms, take advantage of intricate financial arrangements, and use their political connections.

The Genovese family has made significant use of labor racketeering tactics, one of which has been the appointment of devoted allies to important union posts. These people, who often have spotless criminal histories, represent the union in public while covertly carrying out the wishes of the crime family. This strategy has made it more difficult for law enforcement to establish a clear connection between illegal activity and the family, enabling their influence to endure despite heightened scrutiny.

Beyond the short-term financial rewards, the family's labor racketeering actions have had far-reaching effects. The Genovese family has been able to influence local and state politics, get advantageous contracts for affiliated enterprises, and even affect national economic policy via dominating unions. The corruption that resulted has had a knock-on impact on the whole economy, raising consumer prices, decreasing worker safety, and weakening lawful union activity.

Another significant revenue stream for the Genovese criminal family is gambling. The terrain of this illicit industry has altered due to the emergence of legal gaming choices, but the family has shown extraordinary adaptation in continuing to run successful illegal gambling enterprises.

The Genovese family has a long history of engaging in illegal lotteries, sports betting, and number rackets. These activities were often conducted out of front-facing establishments like newsstands, pubs, and social clubs. The family was able to establish a near monopoly on illegal gambling in certain locations because of their geographical control over many neighborhoods, which enabled them to make enormous profits with very little cost.

The Genovese family modified their gaming activities in response to growing pressure from law authorities and the proliferation of legitimate gambling choices. A significant tactic has been the shift to virtual gaming platforms. The family has been able to provide illicit betting alternatives to a large consumer base while lowering the danger of discovery by collaborating with offshore gambling websites. These internet businesses often conceal the transfer of money back to the family by using intricate networks of middlemen and money laundering strategies.

One of the most profitable parts of the Genovese family's gambling ventures is still sports betting. Illegal wagers on major sports, like the World Series or the Super Bowl, may bring in millions of dollars. A network of bookmakers, runners, and enforcers who oversee bet collecting and winning payouts are often involved in the family's activities. One essential element of these operations is still the use of violence or the threat of violence to recover debts from losing bettors.

Genovese family-run casinos have always included high-stakes poker games. These games, which are often hosted in upscale settings and attract affluent patrons, may bring in a sizable sum of money for the family. Apart from sharing earnings, these games often function as networking platforms, enabling relatives and friends to establish links with significant figures in the commercial and political spheres.

It has also been reported that the Genovese family manipulates legitimate gaming businesses to their advantage. This has included plans to embezzle money from Atlantic City's casinos and other places under their sway. The family has been able to embezzle money and rig games by putting friends in important positions at casinos or by influencing current staff members.

Extortion and loan sharking together make up the third main pillar of the Genovese family's illicit activities. Usury, another name for this practice, is the practice of lending money at astronomical interest rates, often to those who are unable to get loans via the proper channels. The victims of the family's loan sharking activities have included small company owners, gamblers, and other crooks in need of fast money.

The loan-sharking activities of the Genovese family are renowned for their effectiveness and brutality. These illicit loans sometimes have yearly interest rates of over 100%, and borrowers are required to make weekly "vig" payments only to pay the interest. When payments are not made on time, it often leads to threats, physical harm, or the forced relinquishment of personal or commercial property.

One of the family's regular strategies for loan sharking is to target those who owe money from gaming. The family may put people in a vicious cycle of debt and exploitation by providing loans to cover gambling losses, often using the same means they use to conduct their illicit gambling enterprises. Their gaming and loan-sharking businesses work well together, and this has been very beneficial for the company.

Loan sharks from the Genovese family have historically targeted small company owners. Economic downturns, company seasonal variations, or unforeseen needs may prompt these people to look for hasty loans, leaving them open to abuse. After being indebted to the family, these company owners often find themselves in a difficult situation where they must continue to make payments or face losing their jobs.

The family's extortion and loan sharking activities often cross over. Companies that take out loans from the Genovese family could face pressure to buy products or services from businesses under Genovese control, to let the family launder money via their enterprise, or to give up a portion of their earnings. This weaves a web of control that victims may find hard to break free from.

The Genovese family has long engaged in extortion as a means of making money for themselves, a practice they have refined over time. It may be combined with loan sharking or carried out independently. Their extortion operations have targeted a diverse array of victims, ranging from sophisticated scams targeting huge companies to street-level shakedowns of small enterprises.

A traditional method of extortion used by Genovese families has been the "protection" racket. Companies operating in areas under family control are compelled to pay regularly for theft, vandalism, and other types of harassment. Due to greater law enforcement attention, the overt violence linked with these scams has diminished recently, although the practice still exists in more covert forms.

The Genovese family has targeted the construction sector specifically for extortion. The family has been able to pressure contractors into paying for "labor peace" or risk project delays, equipment damage, or worker strikes by using their influence over labor unions and important suppliers. These plans have increased the price of building projects by millions of dollars, not only in New York City but also elsewhere.

The Genovese family's extortion practices have also spread into more complex areas. For instance, the family has a history of manipulating stock prices or using insider knowledge to blackmail company leaders via the use of dishonest authorities or business relationships. Even though they are less obvious than typical street-level actions, these white collar extortion tactics may be quite lucrative.

The family has also updated their extortion methods to the internet era in recent years. The organization's cybercrime sections have attacked organizations and companies with ransomware, among other types of digital extortion. These actions show how the family can adapt their illegal businesses to advancements in technology.

Not only are the Genovese family's illegal activities in gambling, extortion, loan sharking, and labor racketeering profitable, but they are also well-connected. A robust and flexible criminal ecology is produced when efforts in one area are supported or made possible by success in another. For instance, having control over labor unions opens doors for money laundering, information collection, influence growth into legal enterprises and political arenas, and even for embezzlement and bribes.

The family's connections to other criminal groups are also part of this connection. Despite its reputation for independence and power, the Genovese family has forged strategic alliances with other mafia families and transnational criminal organizations. The family has been able to penetrate new illicit sectors and expand geographically through these contacts.

The enduring existence and development of these illicit ventures despite continuous law enforcement endeavors attest to the organizational resilience and suppleness of the Genovese family. Even though well-publicized prosecutions have sometimes interfered with their business, the family has continuously shown that they can get back up and go on.

The Genovese family's illicit actions have an effect that goes well beyond the people who are directly harmed by them. The rights and safety of workers have been compromised by labor union corruption. Numerous people have experienced financial disaster and addiction due to their gambling enterprises. Legitimate enterprises and economic progress have been impeded by loan sharking and extortion. Overall, the result has been a steady erosion of social structures and a strain on the economy.

Law enforcement tactics have changed, and with them, the Genovese family's strategies for evading capture and conviction. The use of front organizations, cutouts, and intricate financial plans has made it more and more difficult to link illegal earnings to the family's top officials. Even though it has partially loosened recently, the family's long-standing omertà rule of silence still presents difficulties for prosecutors looking to bring charges against the organization's highest executives.

Prospects and obstacles await the criminal operations of the Genovese family. The family is forced to look for new ways to conceal their illicit profits since conventional money laundering procedures are becoming more challenging due to increased regulatory monitoring of financial institutions. The family has shown interest in these sectors, and the emergence of cryptocurrencies and other financial innovations offers new avenues for money laundering and illicit activity.

How the Genovese family's illegal businesses develop in the future will probably depend on how the world economy and technology environment continue to change. The family may gradually resort to more sophisticated white-collar crimes, cybercrime, or expansion into other geographic regions when certain classic rackets become less lucrative or too hazardous. But for the foreseeable future, their primary skills in extortion, gambling, loan sharking, and labor racketeering—developed over decades of operation—will probably continue to be important components of their criminal portfolio.

Chapter 9

Law Enforcement Efforts and Major Cases

The Genovese criminal family and law enforcement have been engaged in a decades-long struggle that has seen both sides experience major successes and losses. The landscape of organized crime in America has been formed by this continuous conflict, which has also had significant effects on the criminal justice system.

The Valachi Hearings in 1963 were one of the conflict's turning points. The first person to be officially recognized as a member of the American Mafia and to testify about its inner workings was Joseph Valachi, a soldier from the Genovese family. The criminal underworld was rocked by Valachi's decision to violate the rule of silence, or omertà, and law enforcement gained never-before-seen insight into the composition and workings of organized crime.

The country was enthralled with the Valachi Hearings, which took place before the US Senate Permanent Subcommittee on Investigations. The American people had a peek into the clandestine world of La Cosa Nostra for the first time. Valachi highlighted the Mafia's hierarchical structure, the steps involved in becoming a madman, and the range of illegal actions the group engaged in.

Valachi's evidence especially harmed the Genovese family. He identified Vito Genovese as the family's leader and gave details on a host of other influential figures. Law enforcement found this information to be very significant as it provided a roadmap for future investigations and convictions.

The Valachi Hearings had an effect that went much beyond the initial disclosures. They brought about a sea change in the way the public saw organized crime and fueled police actions directed against the Mafia. Several legislative initiatives aimed at stopping racketeering and other mob-related crimes were spurred by the hearings, which also resulted in greater financing for organized crime investigations.

The Genovese family, despite this setback, showed resilience. Vito Genovese and Vincent "The Chin" Gigante led the family, which subsequently implemented more stringent security protocols and became progressively more clandestine in its activities. In the years ahead, as law enforcement steps up its efforts to combat organized crime, this flexibility will become vital.

The 1985–1986 Commission Trial dealt the Genovese family and the larger Mafia their second serious blow. The leaders of the Five Families of New York City were part of the Commission, the controlling body of the American Mafia, which was the object of this historic lawsuit. The trial was the outcome of an elaborate wiretapping and monitoring program used over an extended period by the FBI.

The creative use of the Racketeer Influenced and Corrupt Organizations (RICO) Act was central to the Commission Trial. RICO, which was passed in 1970, gave prosecutors the ability to go after criminal organizations as a whole as opposed to single acts. This strategy worked especially well against the Mafia's hierarchical organization.

The Genovese family, whom Vincent Gigante represented on the Commission, was directly targeted by this case. Thanks to his well-orchestrated "crazy act," Gigante himself avoided indictment, but other prominent family members did not have the same good fortune. The family's leader, Anthony "Fat Tony" Salerno, was found guilty during the trial.

The heads of the Five Families received 100-year jail terms due to the Commission Trial, which dealt a serious blow to the American Mafia's leadership. The Genovese family had to further shield their real leadership from law enforcement scrutiny after Salerno's conviction, which removed a significant member from their ranks.

Following the Commission Trial, the Genovese family intensified their use of deceit and concealment. More emphasis was placed on Gigante's "crazy act," which consisted of walking about Greenwich Village in a bathrobe and muttering to himself. The purpose of this odd conduct was to persuade law authorities that Gigante had the mental capacity to even manage a criminal organization, much less face trial.

The Genovese family was able to hold onto their status as the most powerful and reclusive of the Five Families despite these defeats. They were able to continue their illegal activities, although with more care, because of their ability to adjust to rising pressure from law authorities and maintain rigorous discipline within their ranks.

Law enforcement continued to work to break up the Genovese family's criminal enterprise in the 1990s. Gigante was charged with racketeering in 1990, but a major point of contention in the case was his mental state. Gigante's attorneys said he was mentally unable to stand trial for seven years, which caused delays and inconvenience for the prosecution.

Finally, Gigante was tried in 1997. He was found guilty of several offenses related to murder plot and racketeering, despite his persistently unpredictable conduct in court. With Gigante's conviction, law enforcement achieved a major win by eliminating the Genovese family's longstanding boss and further undermining the organization's leadership.

But while in jail, Gigante maintained his power over the family's business dealings. Gigante's reign didn't end until 2003, when he entered a guilty plea to charges of obstruction of justice about his decades-long delusion of mental illness. This guilty plea was essentially an acknowledgment that his "crazy act" had been a premeditated ruse to get out from under investigation.

Following Gigante's collapse, the government persisted in applying pressure on the Genovese family by launching several charges and prosecutions against members of the organization at different levels. Technological developments in monitoring and enhanced law enforcement agency collaboration facilitated these endeavors.

The indictment of more than 70 Genovese family members and allies on different racketeering counts in 2001 was one such example. The family's activities in the construction business, unions, and illegal gambling were the focus of this broad accusation. The case demonstrated the family's enduring power in these well-established mafia strongholds despite years of pressure from the authorities.

The family's influence on Wall Street and other financial sectors came under further scrutiny in the early 2000s. Several members and associates of the Genovese family were charged in 2003 for their alleged participation in a stock fraud scam that made millions of dollars. The family's capacity to modify its illicit activities to commit more complex financial crimes was shown in this instance.

Despite victories for law enforcement, the Genovese family showed extraordinary fortitude. In contrast to some other Five Families that saw prominent defections and a series of compliant witnesses, the Genovese family maintained their rule of silence. Because of this commitment, it was hard for prosecutors to go to the top of the organization and overthrow the leadership.

Daniel Leo, the family's acting head in the mid-2000s, provided clear evidence of their capacity to shield its senior leadership from prosecution. Even though Leo was ultimately found guilty of racketeering in 2008, the organization's general structure remained substantially intact since the prosecution was unable to establish a case against other prominent family members.

The conviction of Tino Fiumara, a formidable capo who had long dominated the family's activities in the Garden State, in 2008 inflicted a serious blow to the family's operations in New Jersey. Due to her conviction on accusations of racketeering, Fiumara lost a significant source of revenue and a vital member of the family's leadership.

There were many instances in the late 2000s and early 2010s that aimed to undermine the family's ongoing power inside labor unions. Several members and associates of the Genovese family faced charges in 2010 due to their involvement in managing a local branch of the International Longshoremen's Association. This case demonstrated the family's continued ability to use unions for financial gain despite increasing scrutiny.

2016 saw the filing of a broad indictment against 46 suspected mobsters from several criminal organizations, including important members of the Genovese organization, which marked a significant legal victory against the family. This long-term investigation that included cooperative witnesses and intensive monitoring led to the indictment, which included allegations of extortion, illicit gambling, and health care fraud.

Pasquale "Patsy" Parrello and Eugene "Rooster" O'nofrio, who were both allegedly prominent members of the Genovese family, were among those indicted. The indictment described a criminal organization that had kept many of its old rackets in place while adapting to the 21st century.

The 2016 case was especially noteworthy since it included members of all Five Families in addition to the Philadelphia crime family and the Genovese family. This concerted effort was a response from law enforcement to their realization that the Mafia continued to pose a danger to public safety even after years of punishment.

Law enforcement's attention has been drawn more and more in recent years to the family's participation in more contemporary crimes, including identity theft and cybercrime. A number of Genovese family members were accused in 2018 of operating a sophisticated internet gambling enterprise that used offshore servers to avoid discovery.

The family's ongoing participation in conventional rackets has also continued to be the target of law enforcement investigations. A large lawsuit in 2019 focused on the family's dominance of the trash management sector in several areas of New Jersey and New York. This inquiry showed that the Genovese family continued to have a significant influence in this profitable industry even after decades of convictions.

In 2020, one of the family's most significant legal issues occurred when many prominent members were charged with racketeering, extortion, and illicit gambling in an indictment. The use of sophisticated electronic monitoring, such as wiretaps and covert cameras, to establish evidence against the family's leaders made this case noteworthy.

Throughout these several prosecutions, the Genovese family has continuously shown that they are resilient and adaptable. The Genovese organization has maintained a large portion of its authority and illegal activities throughout the years, in contrast to some of the other Five Families, whose power has been greatly reduced.

There are several reasons for this resiliency. Because of the family's insistence on discipline and secrecy, it has been difficult for law enforcement to infiltrate its higher echelons. Additionally, the group has shown an amazing capacity to modify its illegal operations in response to shifting conditions, branching out into new criminal domains while clinging to established rackets.

Furthermore, the family has acted as a barrier to law enforcement initiatives thanks to its extensive network of allies and dishonest authorities. High-ranking family members have been ousted via legal action, but this hasn't stopped the family from promoting from within and carrying on with little interruption.

Both the Genovese family and law enforcement have benefited greatly from the continuous game of cat and mouse. Because of the family's tenacity, law enforcement now has to use more advanced investigation methods and a coordinated strategy to take on organized crime.

On the other hand, the Genovese family has been compelled to operate even more cautiously and secretively due to ongoing pressure from law police. Gone are the days when flashy mafia leaders would publicly show off their money and power; in their place is a more understated strategy meant to deflect suspicion.

The family's defense strategies have changed with the methods used by law enforcement. Gathering evidence and constructing cases against family members has become increasingly difficult for investigators due to the use of Bitcoin, encrypted conversations, and other technical tools.

Law enforcement organizations are nonetheless dedicated to taking down the Genovese family and other organized crime groups despite these obstacles. The government's persistent efforts to eradicate mob influence from respectable companies and sectors are consistently shown by the many charges and prosecutions that are still pending.

The Genovese family's future is still unknown. Despite their remarkable resilience in the face of decades of law enforcement pressure, they nevertheless confront substantial obstacles because of the continual loss of leadership brought about by prosecutions and natural attrition. It remains to be seen whether the family will be able to keep bringing in new members and uphold its rule of silence in the face of harsh jail terms and plea agreements.

Chapter 10

The Code of Silence: Omertà and Genovese Family Culture

Known as the most powerful and clandestine of New York's Five Families, the Genovese crime family has long upheld the omertà, or strict rule of silence. The family's activities have been built on this philosophy, which is ingrained in their culture and has contributed significantly to their success and longevity in the world of organized crime.

The Italian term omertà, which translates roughly as "code of silence," refers to more than simply the simple prohibition against assisting the authorities. It is a sophisticated system based on loyalty, honor, and independence that originated in southern Italian culture. Omertà has been turned into an art form for the Genovese family, who have built an almost impenetrable wall of secrecy that has thwarted law enforcement operations for decades.

The history of omertà in the Genovese family dates back to the early 1900s, when Giuseppe "the Clutch Hand" Morello was its head. Born in Corleone, Sicily, Morello carried with him the customs of his own country, which included remaining silent and not assisting the police. These values were ingrained in family leadership down the generations, growing more sophisticated and established with every decade that went by.

The significance of omertà was further highlighted under the rule of Charles "Lucky" Luciano, who turned the loosely organized gang into a more systematic criminal business. Luciano realized that the family's capacity to function well rested on its ability to keep its operations under wraps. He taught his followers that it was the worst sin and would cause death to disclose the family's secrets.

But it was Vincent "The Chin" Gigante who brought the Genovese family's genuine skill of omertà to completion. Gigante's notorious "crazy act," whereby he strolled around Greenwich Village in his bathrobe while whispering to himself, was the furthest manifestation of the family's dedication to concealment. For years, Gigante managed the family's affairs while avoiding attention from the police by pretending to be mentally ill. This complex deception was a family-wide effort to safeguard their leader and their company, not simply a personal tactic.

Gigante's model established a new benchmark for the family's omertà practice. It was required of members at all levels to take great measures to keep the family's secrets safe. This included being prepared to forgo cooperation with law enforcement in favor of jail time, to stick to their cover stories in the face of overwhelming evidence, and to sever connections with close friends or family members who would endanger the organization's security.

The Genovese family's omertà devotion went much beyond their outright refusal to engage with government police. It was ingrained in all facets of their relationships and activities. Family members were taught to use coded language while discussing business, to communicate carefully, and to be alert to the prospect of being watched from the moment they joined the company.

A system of incentives and penalties served to further encourage this culture of concealment. In addition to receiving promotions inside the organization and access to more profitable criminal operations, those who showed unflinching devotion and discretion also received more protection from their families. On the other hand, those who were seen as being careless or loose-lipped suffered harsh repercussions, which may include bodily harm in addition to a decline in rank and money.

The family did not just adhere to omertà among its adopted members. It was also required of associates—criminals working with the family but not officially inducted—to adhere to the rule of silence. This wider circle of devoted friends and supporters offered the Genovese family even more protection from the authorities' attention.

The Genovese family's omertà dedication was most evident in the way they handled internal conflicts. The Genovese family chose to resolve disputes discreetly and inside the family, in contrast to some other mafia families who occasionally resorted to violent public displays as a means of dispute resolution. This kept the family's reputation of power and togetherness intact and reduced the possibility of drawing unwelcome attention from police authorities or other criminal groups.

The family's commitment to privacy permeated their digital use as well. The Genovese family changed the way they communicated as electronic monitoring advanced in sophistication. They were known to use a range of strategies to avoid being monitored electronically, including wiretaps. These included talking in code during calls, meeting in person to discuss difficult topics in safe spaces, and using pay phones rather than personal phones.

The success of the Genovese family's omertà strategy is perhaps best shown by the very small number of senior members who have come out as informants over time. The Genovese family has held together rather well, in contrast to other mafia families that have been shaken by high-profile defections. This family's tenacity in the face of severe law enforcement pressure is evidence of how deeply its members adhere to the rule of silence and how strong their culture is.

But upholding such a rigid rule of silence is not without its difficulties. The organization may become paranoid due to the ongoing watchfulness needed to maintain omertà. Members must be on the lookout for any informants and law enforcement personnel who may be hiding. Besides straining family ties, this climate of constant distrust may hinder effective corporate operations.

Furthermore, the family's determination to keep things secret might sometimes make it more difficult for them to grow into new criminal territory or attract new members. Instead of abiding by the strict code of behavior enforced by the Genovese family, young, aspirational criminals can be lured to other groups that offer faster routes to money and prestige.

The Genovese family's dedication to omertà has endured despite these difficulties. This is largely because the family's leadership has always placed a high value on loyalty and secrecy. From Gigante's complex deception to the more modern tactic of enlisting "street bosses" to shield the real leadership from discovery, the family has shown to be very adept at changing its ways without compromising its essential beliefs.

The family's accomplishments have further strengthened their commitment to omertà. The Genovese family's ability to hold onto its dominance as the most potent mafia group in the United States in the face of tremendous pressure from law enforcement is a compelling example of how successful their strategy is. This achievement, in turn, strengthens the members' conviction that rigorous observance of the rule of silence is advantageous in addition to obligatory.

The Genovese family has an omertà culture that goes beyond their dealings with the police. It also sets the rules for how members communicate with one another and the outside world. It is expected of family members to keep a low profile and abstain from ostentatious displays of wealth or power that might draw unwelcome attention. This is in sharp contrast to certain other mafia personalities who have openly shown their criminality or courted media attention.

The family's commercial activities also exhibit this understated style. The Genovese family engages in a variety of illegal operations, ranging from classic rackets like loan sharking and gambling to more complex financial crimes, but they often run these businesses with a level of secrecy that distinguishes them from their competitors. By taking this cautious approach, the family has been able to minimize their vulnerability to law enforcement investigation while maintaining its criminal enterprise.

The Genovese family's stance on violence has also been shaped by their adherence to omertà. Although there is little doubt that the family is capable of utilizing force when required, they usually prefer to settle disputes amicably via discussion or coercion. This circumspect attitude toward violence is a calculated decision as much as a moral one. Every violent act bears the potential of drawing attention from police authorities, something the family tries to stay away from.

Induction rituals are part of the family's tradition of keeping things private. The ceremony of being accepted into the family is a momentous occasion, yet it is carried out with the highest secrecy. In contrast to several other mafia families, whose induction ceremony details have been made public by informants, the Genovese family has maintained the secrecy surrounding the contents of their ceremony.

There have been expenses associated with this concealment devotion. The psychological effects of family members having to maintain omertà all the time may be severe. Stress and paranoia might result from the desire to always watch what one says and does and to be alert for any risks. Some participants have compared the experience to being in a constant state of combat and always on the lookout for possible adversaries.

Furthermore, the family's emphasis on privacy may make it more difficult for them to defend themselves in court or against claims made in public. Negative narratives about the family's actions are sometimes allowed to remain unquestioned since the family declines to defend against claims in public or interact with the media. This may affect not just how the public views the case but also how the case is handled in court since the prosecution can present their case without facing a lot of opposition from the family.

The omertà tradition of the Genovese family has also had to change in response to shifting legal and technical environments. The family's capacity to maintain its curtain of secrecy has been tested by the growth of electronic monitoring, the growing use of informants by law enforcement, and the enactment of RICO (Racketeer Influenced and Corrupt Organizations Act) regulations.

The family has modified their methods as a result. Information has become more compartmentalized as a result, with members receiving just the bare minimum of details required to do their jobs. Along with embracing new technology that might help with safe communication, the family has also been cautious about any possible weaknesses that these technologies may bring.

The family's ties to other criminal groups have been affected by its dedication to omertà. The Genovese family maintains commercial partnerships and alliances with other mafia families and criminal organizations, however, these dealings are marked by a certain amount of reserve and prudence. The family is cautious about sharing information with its supporters since they are always on the lookout for any leaks or betrayals.

This careful attitude also applies to the family's dealings with respectable companies and public officials. The family has always had a network of contacts in the political and financial spheres, but these links are very discreet. The Genovese family would rather retain its power out of the public eye than some other criminal groups that have tried to build public ties with politicians or business executives.

The Genovese family's culture of omertà is maintained not only by members' constant dread of punishment but also by a set of moral principles that are ingrained in them from the beginning of their membership. Not only are loyalty, honor, and discretion shown as necessary but also as moral qualities. Members are instilled with pride in their capacity to maintain confidentiality and the belief that being silent is a sign of strength and self-control.

The family's internal mythology supports this moral system. Narratives of other members who remained silent in the face of lengthy jail terms or threats to their lives are disseminated as role models to follow. On the other hand, the few cases of individuals who have violated omertà are portrayed as warning stories, their tragic endings acting as a deterrent to those who may consider assisting the police.

Their adherence to omertà has shaped the Genovese family's succession planning strategy. In contrast to some other mafia families, which have occasionally seen public power battles that occur after a boss's death or incarceration, the Genovese family has handled these changes with amazing tact. Even law enforcement often speculates about who the family's senior executives are, which is evidence of how successful their concealment procedures are.

The Genovese family has been able to preserve a level of stability that has escaped some of its competitors because of this culture of concealment. Over the years, the family has weathered periods of severe law enforcement scrutiny and leadership changes without major damage to operations by eschewing public power conflicts and putting up a unified front.

The Genovese family's omertà tradition is still developing as the group encounters new difficulties. The family's capacity to keep things under wraps might be threatened by several factors, including the growth of cybercrime and digital monitoring, shifting public perceptions of organized crime, and improved police enforcement tactics. But in keeping with its past, the family keeps evolving, coming up with fresh approaches to preserve its long-standing custom of quiet in the face of these contemporary difficulties.

Chapter 11

The Genovese Family's Influence on Popular Culture

With their illustrious past and infamous reputation, the Genovese crime family has had a lasting impact on popular culture. The family's impact has been felt in a variety of media, including music, television, cinema, and literature. Audiences have been captivated by stories of power, devotion, and the murky side of American culture.

The early years of organized crime in America may be linked to the Genovese family's appeal to popular culture. The Genovese organization, one of the Five Families of New York City, has always piqued the interest of authors, filmmakers, and artists who want to delve further into the intricate realm of the Mafia. The family has always been the most powerful criminal organization in the United States, making it a very interesting topic for imaginative interpretation. It is also known for its strict discipline and secrecy.

Mario Puzo's novels provided one of the first and most important representations of the Genovese family in popular culture. Many aspects of the fictional Corleone family were influenced by real-life Mafia leaders, notably those from the Genovese organization, even though Puzo's famous book "The Godfather" and its following film adaptations were not directly based on the Genovese family. Particularly, Frank Costello, a former Genovese family leader renowned for his political ties and somewhat civilized manner, was compared to Vito Corleone.

The Genovese family had a greater impact on "The Godfather" than just serving as inspiration for characters. Many of the organizational tenets and rules of behavior that characterized the Genovese family were shown in the book and the films, including the value placed on family loyalty, the significance of political connections, and the use of respectable companies as fronts for illicit activity. Even though they weren't exclusive to the Genovese family, these components were closely linked to their strategy and influenced how the general public saw organized crime.

The cultural phenomenon "The Godfather" led to a resurgence of interest in Mafia-related narratives in all media. The Genovese family's standing in popular culture profited from this tendency, as authors and filmmakers looked into the real-life sources of inspiration for the fictitious depictions. With the

Genovese organization often taking center stage because of its image as the most powerful and secretive of the organizations, documentaries, books, and television series started to dive further into the history and activities of the Five Families.

"Goodfellas," a 1990 Martin Scorsese film, solidified the Genovese family's status in popular culture even further. The film contained several characters and narrative points that were inspired by Genovese family members and connections, even if its main emphasis was the Lucchese criminal family. Paul Sorvino's portrayal of Paul Cicero was modeled on Paul Vario, a capo from the Lucchese family with strong connections to the Genovese mafia. The way the Mafia was portrayed in the movie—complete with its hierarchical structure and rule of silence—was quite similar to how the Genovese family operated.

Another major factor influencing how the general public views the Genovese family is television. The highly acclaimed television series "The Sopranos," which lasted from 1999 to 2007, combined features evocative of the Genovese organization with themes drawn from the history and culture of the DeCavalcante criminal family in New Jersey. Many of the difficulties experienced by the actual Genovese family in the late 20th and early 21st centuries were mirrored in the show's portrayal of the Mafia's struggles to hold onto power in a changing society, as well as its examination of the psychological toll of running a criminal empire.

The longtime leader of the Genovese family, Vincent "The Chin" Gigante, had several characteristics with Dominic Chianese's portrayal of Junior Soprano. Gigante gained notoriety for his "crazy act," which had him pacing the streets of New York while wearing a bathrobe and muttering to himself to get away with it. Sometimes Junior Soprano would behave in a way that reflected this quirky behavior, especially in later seasons of the program as the character's mental health started to decline.

The Genovese family's impact on popular culture went beyond their fictional representations. The family's history and activities have been a recurring theme in true crime books and films, giving readers a look into the real-life counterpart of the Mafia empires they had grown to know in fiction. Books like James B. Jacobs' "The Genovese Family" and Selwyn Raab's "Five Families" provide in-depth descriptions of the group's ascent to prominence and continued influence in American organized crime.

These nonfiction books helped to further mythologize the Genovese family while simultaneously educating readers about the reality of organized crime. The family's continuing public interest was further cemented by the gripping stories of intricate criminal businesses, political corruption, and the cat-and-mouse game between law enforcement and mobsters, which captured the attention of readers and viewers.

The legend surrounding the Genovese family and the broader world of organized crime have also had an impact on the music business. Many musicians from a variety of genres have made references to the Mafia in their songs, often taking cues from the imagined danger and glitz of the lifestyle. Even if these allusions don't necessarily relate directly to the Genovese family, they do add to the Mafia mythology's broader cultural influence, of which the Genovese organization is a major component.

Mafia images and narratives have been adopted by hip-hop in particular. Mafia themes have been interwoven into the music of artists like Jay-Z, Nas, and The Notorious B.I.G., who often draw comparisons between the world of organized crime and the street life they encountered. Representing the height of underworld dominance and prosperity, the Genovese family has functioned as a touchstone for this kind of tale, being one of the most potent and long-lasting criminal families.

The family has had a significant impact on popular culture outside American media. The Genovese group and its equivalents have been an inspiration for several international motion pictures and television programs. While centering on other criminal organizations, Italian crime dramas such as "Gomorrah" and "Suburra" include aspects evocative of the structure and activities of the Genovese family. The mystique surrounding American organized crime has been exported to a worldwide audience thanks to these performances, which has strengthened the Genovese family's standing in popular culture.

Another medium in which the cultural impact of the Genovese family may be seen is via video games. The hugely successful "Grand Theft Auto" video game series, especially "Grand Theft Auto IV," showcased made-up criminal groups that were modeled around New York's Five Groups. The group action of organized crime in the game, which included territorial conflicts, hierarchical systems, and the balance between legal and illicit industries, was largely inspired by the real-life activities of families like the Genovese organization.

The family has influenced fashion and lifestyle besides entertainment in popular culture. The increased public perception of Mafia members, particularly those from the Genovese family, is largely responsible for the "gangster chic" look, which is defined by sharp suits, fedoras, and an aura of deadly elegance. Celebrities and the general public have adopted this look, which has affected fashion trends and strengthened the cultural cachet of images of organized crime.

Real-world implications have resulted from the Genovese family's obsession with popular culture. There have sometimes been complaints that the idealized depiction of Mafia life in the media elevates illegal activity and hides the actual extent of organized crime's influence on society. Discussions about the accountability of media creators and artists for their portrayals of criminal groups have been triggered by this.

Many artists contend, however, that their creations serve as warning stories, highlighting the moral emptiness and eventual demise of those who chose a life of crime. They argue that a detailed examination of topics like loyalty, family, power, and the American Dream is made possible by the intricate depictions of Mafia leaders, who are often influenced by members of the Genovese family.

The way that the public and law enforcement see organized crime has also been affected by the Genovese family's cultural influence. The media's portrayal of the family as smart and reclusive has added to the family's mystique and sometimes made attempts to stop their illegal operations more difficult. A romanticized picture of the organization's activities has sometimes resulted from the public's interest, which is fed by how it is portrayed in popular culture, possibly hiding the actual nature of its crimes.

In popular culture, organized crime has been portrayed more realistically and nuanced in recent years. This change has made it possible to analyze the Genovese family's legacy and effects on American society more critically. The human cost of organized crime has been the subject of more and more documentaries and theatrical plays, which have examined the repercussions on families, communities, and people entangled in the Mafia's web.

Unexpected manifestations of the Genovese family's cultural influence have also been seen. The rule of silence known as "omertà," which has traditionally been connected to families, is now part of popular culture. These days, the term is often used to denote any rigorous devotion to secrecy or non-cooperation with authorities in situations that are quite different from organized crime. This language adaptation shows how deeply ingrained Mafia ideas—especially those connected to the Genovese family—have become in popular culture.

Pop culture's depiction of the Genovese family has changed along with society's perception of organized crime. Contemporary portrayals often center on the family's adjustment to the times, examining how established criminal organizations deal with the difficulties of the twenty-first century. Stories about cybercrime, international financial manipulation, and the relationship between organized crime and international terrorism have resulted from this.

The family's impact on popular culture is still developing. The representation of organized crime is being reimagined by emerging generations of authors, filmmakers, and artists. Even if the traditional themes of family, power, and devotion are still important, modern art often delves into the psychological complexities of those who are a part of criminal organizations, going beyond straightforward depictions of good and evil.

The Genovese family's cultural influence may be seen in digital media in addition to conventional media. The Genovese family is often at the heart of discussions among fans about the history and legend of organized crime on social media platforms and online forums. The family's mythology has new paths to propagate and develop due to this online interaction, guaranteeing its ongoing relevance in the digital era.

The Genovese family's ongoing interest in popular culture reveals deeper facets of the American mind. The story of the organization's ascent from modest immigrant beginnings to become a strong and significant force, although a darkly warped one, connects with the American Dream. This tale of poverty to riches, together with themes of power struggles and familial devotion, never fails to enthrall viewers and inspire artistic endeavors.

The Genovese family is going to have a big impact on popular culture for as long as people are interested in tales about crime, power, and the unseen forces that affect society. Its projected and actual history offers artists plenty of material to work with, guaranteeing that the family's influence on our cultural environment will last for many years.

www.ingramcontent.com/pod-product-compliance
Lightning Source LLC
Chambersburg PA
CBHW050310230526
45471CB00005B/2107